The History of Deaf People

A Source Book

daufr

DEAF HISTORY

Per Eriksson

Translated from the Swedish by James Schmale

The Swedish original, *Dövas Historia, en faktasamling.* Del 1, was published by SIH Läromedel, the Learning Materials Division of the National Swedish Agency for Special Education in 1993.

Address:
Daufr
Räntmästargatan 85
SE-702 25 Örebro
SWEDEN

Telefax: ++46 19 12 53 02
E-mail: daufr@hotmail.com

TRYCKMAKARNA i Örebro AB, 1998
ISBN 91-630-6822-2

The cover shows the oldest known color wall chart of the finger-spelling alphabet, Vadstena School for Older Deaf Students 1878 to 1902. National Archives, Vadstena, Sweden.

This book is dedicated to the memory of my mother, Eva.

Contents

Foreword

The advantage of The History of Deaf People, A Source Book is that it is just that: a collection of facts. Teachers can use it to plan classes in the history of the deaf at schools for the deaf. We have needed a book like this for a long time.

Deaf clubs will find The History of Deaf People, A Source Book useful as the basis for deaf history classes for adults, for instance evening classes. It will also be of great help to government and municipal officials in their efforts to improve education for the deaf and severely hearing impaired.

In his book, A Hundred Years in Sweden, Sven Aspling quotes Sweden´s former Prime Minister, Tage Erlander as saying that the older he gets, the more convinced he becomes that today´s problems cannot be solved without a sound understanding of the past. Per Eriksson´s Source Book gives us and public administrators a long-awaited comprehensive overview of deaf people´s history.

Lars H. Kruth

Introduction

I am deaf and grew up in the fifties, at the time when the Wedenberg oral method prevailed in Swedish deaf education. I spent part of my elementary school years in a special class for the hearing impaired, and part as the only deaf student in an otherwise all-hearing class.

In 1970, I encountered the world of the deaf and became interested in learning sign language and its grammar. I was told there was no printed material in this area. No one had a grasp of the technicalities of sign language at that time as no research had yet been conducted ; nor was there any modern book on the history of deaf people.

In 1979, I was elected officer of the Örebro County Deaf Club and gradually gained a better understanding of the deaf community and its culture.

That same year, a collection of old books and periodicals about the deaf was bequeathed to the Associatio1n by the estate of Hilding Zommarin, former principal of the school for the deaf.

In the mid-eighties, the deaf community started to take an interest in the documentation of its history. This was done in various ways: by gathering material by or about deaf people, organizing evening classes and interviewing people on video. However, what deaf historical material there was fragmentary and scattered in diffe-rent parts Sweden.

I became increasingly aware of the need to compile a history of the deaf focusing on deaf education. Since my home is in Örebro, I have concentrated on central Sweden, visiting various archives, perusing books and discussing the subject with other enthusiasts. My aim was to compile a source book, primarily for use as a complement to work on this subject in schools for the deaf.

A book like this can never be quite complete; the more research one does, the more interesting facts come to light. One major obstacle to my research was the fact that deaf community periodicals are not available on microfilm. For this reason, I have very little of that kind of material here. For further study, I recommend the books listed in my bibliography and a visit to historical archives, for instance at schools for the deaf.

I would like to thank Tord Lind of Örebro for encouraging me to expand my notes into a book and the National Swedish Association of the Deaf and its chairman Anders Andersson for the financial support I received for the work on this book. I would also like to thank Lars Kruth, Claes G. Olsson and Bo Andersson for their suggestions and for having reviewed the material for this book. Lastly, I wish to thank the Örebro County Deaf Club for its support and cooperation.

I have endeavored to modernize the language of my sources, replacing the archaic "deaf and dumb" with "deaf". However, most direct quotations are in the original form and only in the case of long references have I chosen a more modern vocabulary. It was difficult to determine the accuracy of such terms as "gestural language, symbols, dactylology, finger language, positions of the fingers". Today, the term sign language is universal. In many cases I have chosen to leave the archaic terms unaltered in this source book.

Per Eriksson
Örebro
January, 1991

The Evolution of the Swedish Word "Döv" (Deaf)

In the Indo-European languages, a language group to which the Germanic languages belong, words are formed or inflected by the processes of umlaut or ablaut, i.e. changes in the vowel sounds. The quantitative aspect of vowels can also be altered: they can change from short to long, long to short, or be completely deleted.

From the Indo-European stem *dhubh* the Germanic languages have evolved the adjective **dauða*, the Old Norse variant of which became **daubhaR* in the masculine nominative singular.

The asterisk(*)in front of the word means that the form given is a reconstruction based on what is known of the phonetic evolution of the Germanic languages.

The symbol ð and the letters *bh* are two different ways of writing the same sound, something in between b and v.

The earliest actual record of the word is from the second half of the thirteenth century.

The word *döv* (deaf), having been passed down from Old Germanic, has always been included in the vocabulary of the Swedish language.

daubhaR - The Old Norse form is *daubhaR*.

daufr - During the Viking era it evolved into *daufr* (the f is pronounced "v")

döver - Sometime in the tenth or eleventh century the word became *döver* (the ending -er for the masculine nominative singular).

The oldest meaning of the word was dazed or confused.

Deyvur, the Faeroese word for deaf, also means slow to come to a boil (of the contents of a pot) while *daufur,* an archaic form of the Icelandic word for deaf, meant weak, worn out, dejected, drained (of strength), sluggish, dull.

The fact that we find the meaning of non-hearing, not only in the Swedish word *döv,* but also in its etymological relatives, the other Scandinavian languages (Danish *døv,* Icelandic *daufr,* etc.) as well as in the rest of the Germanic languages (German *taub,* English *deaf,* etc.) indicates that the word acquired this meaning long before the early Middle Ages when Swedish became a separate language.

Both the form and meaning of the word döv have been a part of the vocabulary of the Swedish language for a very long time.

The Word "Dövstum" in Sweden

Only fairly recently did the word *dövstum* become a part of the Swedish vocabulary. The first written record containing this compound is from the year 1799. Linguistic critics of the time discarded the word as not genuinely Swedish. *Dövstum* is a translation of the German word, *taubstumm,* which appears in texts in Germany around the year 1734. The Swedish word, *döv* has never connoted stupidity, though historically, the English word *dumb* also meant mute, hence deaf and dumb.

While the compounds *taubstumm, deaf-mute, sourd-muet,* and *sordo-mudo* could be found in other languages, a similar compound was not introduced into Swedish until later. In the eighteenth century the most common written forms were *döfve dumbar, döfva och dumma*, or simply *dumbar*, i.e. mutes. The singular form was *dumbe* or *dum*. In the nineteenth century the compound *döfstum* appeared and as a result of the 1906 orthographic revision of the Swedish language, its correct spelling became *dövstum*.

In the year 1886, Johan August Wilén, principal of the school for the deaf in Uppsala, wrote the pamphlet *Facts and Advice*. He proves to be a man of exceptionally modern ideas for his time. This is especially clear in points 16 and 17 where he argues for a revision in terminology, replacing *dövstum* with simply *döv* ("deaf" instead of "deaf and dumb"). We were to wait many more years before this bit of advice was officially accepted.

Wilén´s Facts and Advice

to the parents and guardians of deaf and dumb children, and to public authorities with professional contact with deaf and dumb children.

1. A child who, due to deafness or deficient hearing, is unable to communicate with others, is is termed deaf and dumb.

2. This deafness or hardness of hearing may be either from birth or the result of disease in the first, second, third, fourth, fifth, sixth or some later year of the child´s life.

3. A child who is born deaf or who has lost his hearing before having learned to speak or before developing a firm grasp of the language, is referred to as genuinely deaf and dumb.

4. A child who has gone deaf after having been able to hear and speak for some time is referred to as not genuinely deaf and dumb.

5. Those of us who are in full possession of our senses learn to speak in babyhood by mimicking what we hear said by our parents, siblings or by other people around us. The genuinely deaf and dumb child, on the other hand, unable to hear anything, has nothing to mimic and therefore does not learn to speak.

6. The not genuinely deaf and dumb person, in that he no longer has access to the model speech of others to help him preserve and further develop his speech, will speak less and less clearly over the years and runs the risk of forgetting it altogether.

7. Since the genuinely deaf and dumb pupil cannot be taught speech with the help of hearing, the media of instruction must be vision (he must read the speech of others from their lips) and the sense of touch (in beginning speech training, he will feel and compare the vibrations of his teacher´s throat with those of his own).

8. Also the not genuinely deaf and dumb student must be instructed by the same methods in order to retain and improve his speech.

9. The first deaf and dumb person to receive instruction — in the eighth century AC — was instructed in speech. In Germany the deaf and dumb have been taught to speak for over a century.

10. *The deaf and dumb have the same speech organs: chest, ribcage, windpipe, mouth and oral parts; thus they have the same potential for speech as those of us who retain all our senses.*

11. *Man has five senses: sight, hearing, smell, taste and touch. There is, however, no sixth sense, one of speech.*

12. *Deafness and poor hearing are the result of an undoubtably incurable defect of the hearing organs, but the inability to speak is by no means of organic origin. It is, instead, the result of outside circumstances which can be more or less remedied, thus facilitating the kind of speech training described above.*

13. *Real muteness only occurs in cases where there is some defect of the speech organs: an enlarged tongue or some malformation of the palate. Such cases are, however, extremely rare.*

J.A. Wilén

14. *In this pamphlet, I am of course referring to those deaf and dumb people who, aside from defective hearing, are normally endowed, both physically and mentally.*

15. *It follows that the reservations of those who regard it as inappropriate to place pupils with some residual speech among deaf and dumb pupils or to send such pupils to schools for the deaf and dumb are entirely unfounded.*

16. *The term "deaf and dumb" is highly inaccurate: a poor term passed down to us from a time when it was still generally believed that deafness and muteness were both due to organic deformity, an antiquated term still in use only by force of habit.*

17. *It would be an improvement to replace the highly inaccurate terms, "deaf and dumb", "teachers for the deaf and dumb", "schools for the deaf and dumb", with the more accurate and appropriate terms, "deaf", "teachers for the deaf" and "schools for the deaf".*

18. *As this change in terminology doubtlessly remains unfeasable, the term "deaf and dumb" should at least be interpreted in so broad a sense as to allow for admission to schools for the deaf and dumb of all children who, because of defective hearing, cannot take part in public education.*

19. *Where else are these unfortunate deaf children to receive their schooling?*

Upsala, January 1886.

National Archives in Gothenburg. Records of The Väner School for the Deaf, Vänersborg.

Government Documentation

In many modern societies counterparts of the term "deaf and dumb" have been abandoned as inaccurate. In the United States, the terms "deaf and dumb", "deaf-mutes" and "mutes" were formerly in use. As new schools started to call themselves simply "schools for the deaf", however, many older schools followed suit. In Germany, the term "Taubstummenschulen" was replaced in the thirties by "Gehörlosenschulen". In Norway, the term "döveskoler" has been in use a long time.

In Sweden, the change from the term, "dövstumskolor" to "dövskolor" is one of the propositions presented in the final report of a government survey conducted in 1945.

Official Government Report (SOU) 1947:64

XXII Suggested Alteration in Wording of Government Regulations for the Education of the Deaf and dumb.

Swedish Government Regulations for Schools for the Deaf

Chapter 1 : Goal and Organization of the Schools

§ 1

The national schools for the deaf aim to develop students both intellectually and physically and raise them to become independent, responsible adults. Utilizing what residual hearing the students have, they should be trained as much as possible in the use of normal language and given a standard of education as close as possible to that of ordinary public schools. Furthermore, students should be given vocational guidance and basic vocational training.

§ 2

Schools for the deaf are preschools, elementary and secondary schools. For the deaf with additional handicaps, there are two training centers and a boarding school.

Special regulations apply for these institutions."

This proposed change in wording meant replacing the term "deaf and dumb" with the more accurate term "deaf". The proposal was rejected at first and the National Board of Education did not officially adopt the term "deaf" until the year 1953. However, the Swedish Association of the Deaf and dumb (*Svenska Dövstumsförbundet*), founded on February 22, 1922, changed its name to the Swedish National Association of the Deaf (*Sveriges Dövas Riksförbund*) in 1950.

For its 1981 Swedish translation of the New Testament, the Bible Commission consulted Sven-Eric Lönnell, pastor for the deaf in Örebro, regarding the use of the words deaf, mute and dumb. In the classical Greek original Lönnell found the following words:

κωφός..... (kofos) = mute, deaf
ἄλαλος.. (alalos) = unable to speak, mute
σιωπάω... (siapao) = to be silent, refrain from speaking
ἄφωνος... (afonos) = without voice

The choice of the appropriate Swedish word was made according to the context of the corresponding Greek word.

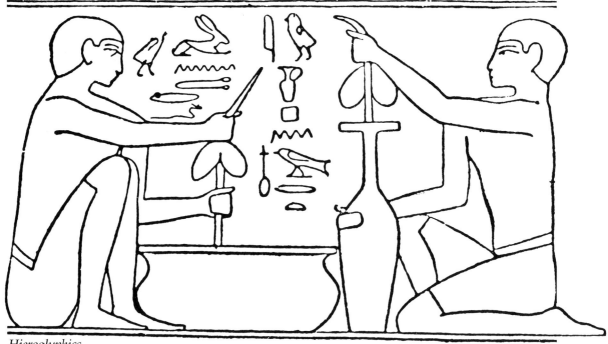

Hieroglyphics

Ancient Egypt

In ancient times Egypt had a highly advanced culture. Papyrus scriptures found in Egyptian tombs date back to centuries before the time of Moses. The deaf were thought to be specially chosen by the gods. Due to the prevailing humanitarian philosophy at the time, the lame and disabled were allowed to live and perhaps even given help. The silence and peculiar behavior of deaf people lent them an air of mysticism. Because the Egyptians regarded the deaf as specially chosen people, they treated them with deference. The deaf were educated in ancient Egypt. There is a certain similarity between hieroglyphs and the gestural language of the deaf. Presumably, hieroglyphs were used to teach the deaf.

Egypt c. 1400 B.C.

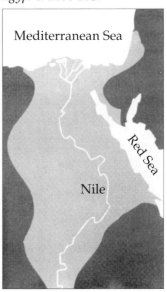

The Deaf Son of King Croesus

The following legend illustrates what mystical powers were attributed to people who deviated in some way from the normal, particularly mutes.

King Croesus of Lydia had a deaf son who could not speak. Croesus had done everything in his power to free his son from this curse. He also sent a messenger to Delphi to ask the oracle there for advice. The Pythian priestess replied, "Mighty king of the land of Lydia, foolish Croesus, for so many years you have longed to hear your son´s cheerful greetings. Relinquish your longing. Far better be it for you never to see that grievous day when your son breaks his silence!"

When Cyrus defeated King Croesus in 546 BC, strict orders were given that Croesus was to be taken prisoner, but not executed. When a Persian soldier, not realizing who his prisoner was, was about to slay Croesus, the prince´s tongue was freed by horror and he cried, "Man, do not slay Croesus!" Those were the first

Seated Pythian Priestess

words he uttered. The reason for this may have been that his tongue was loosened by the shock of seeing his father in mortal danger. For the rest of his life after that he could speak. King Croesus´ life was spared and Lydia became part of the Persian kingdom under the rule of Cyrus.

The Oldest Known Mention of Sign Language

In ancient Greece, Plato (427-347 BC) in his dialogue "Cratylus", mentions the deaf who express themselves in gestures och movements, depicting that which is light or of a higher sphere by raising the hand or describing a galloping horse by imitating its motion.

Plato was a student of Socrates (dead 399 BC) whom he quotes in Cratylus as saying:

Lydia - Persia

13

If we had neither voice nor tongue, and yet wished to manifest things to one another, should we not, like those which are at present mute, endeavour to signify our meaning by the hands, head, and other parts of the body? ... I think, therefore, that if we wished to signify that which is upwards and light, we should raise our hands towards the heaven, imitating the nature of the thing itself; but that if we wished to indicate things downwards and heavy, we should point with our hands to the earth ...

Wright, David. Deafness, a Personal Account. Allen Lane the Penguin Press. London 1969. p. 156.

The Greeks

In ancient Greece, in the two centuries before Christ, the plight of the deaf was hard. The people of ancient Greece were educated and aesthetically inclined. Works of sculpture from this era bear witness to this.

Because societies were constantly at war or involved in armed conflict with one another, physical and mental prowess were regarded as essential characteristics. All ugliness or deviation was viewed with contempt. Every man was meant to serve the state.

Sparta was at that time a war-waging state where the classes in power purposefully reared their youths to be soldiers. According to the Spartan laws of Lykuros (ninth century BC) all children in any way crippled were to be murdered at birth. In Athens this was also the fate of deaf babies in accordance with the laws

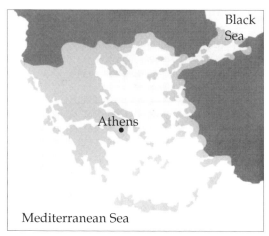

Greece

of Solon the Wise, an Athenean statesman and bard who lived around 600 BC. He regarded the extermination of all individuals who would in any way be a burden to society as being in the best interests of the state.

The reasons for muteness were unknown in early times. The Greek philosopher, Aristotle (384-322 BC) noted that muteness was often linked with deafness: "Those who are born deaf all become speechless, they have a voice, but are destitute of speech." (*History of Animals* IV. ix).

Aristotle could find no explanation for the muteness of the deaf. His theory was that the deaf lacked reason, making educating them an impossible task. In the year 355 BC Aristotle was the first to examine deafness and its consequences more closely.

Galen, a Greek physician from Pergamum (c. 131 to c. 201 AD) presented the theory that speech and hearing had the same source in the brain. If one of these functions was damaged, the other must also be affected. Speech and hearing went hand in hand. Consequently, the deaf could never learn to speak. The writings of Aristotle and Galen went unquestioned until as late as the sixteenth century AD when the assumption that the deaf are uneducable was finally challenged.

The Dogma of Aristotle

Aristotle (384-322 BC) believed that everything that is to reach the human consciousness must enter it through one of the organs of perception.

Lennart Andersson (1990) quotes, "If one of the senses is lacking, it necessarily follows that a certain type of understan-

Aristotle

ding is also lacking, an understanding impossible to acquire." Aristotle regarded hearing as the most important channel of learning and assumed that it must be more difficult to provide the deaf with a culitivated manner than the blind.

For centuries, Aristotle´s verdict that the deaf were entirely untrainable remained unquestioned. Aristotle was regarded all this time as an infallible scientific authority. No physician dared to contest his dogma.

The only issue under debate was the connection between deafness and muteness. Anatomists from antiquity until the renaissance assumed the facial and aural nerves were connected in the brain and that a defect in one nerve would automatically affect the other. Deafness was believed to be inseparably linked to the inablity to speak.

Thomas Willis (1621-75) discovered the role of the cochlea in hearing.

Aristotle´s assumption was challenged by Johann Bohn (1640-1718), who, in his *Circulus Anatomico-Psysiologicus* (Leipzig 1686) refuted the theory that deaf and dumbness was caused by a connection of the facial and aural nerves. This put an end to the dispute about the origins of deaf-muteness. For a long time after this, nothing appeared in medical literature on the issue of deaf-muteness.

Note: The facial nerve is the seventh cerebral nerve; the aural nerve the eighth.

The Romans

During the Roman era, particularly in its early years, the lives of deaf people were extremely difficult. The head of a Roman family wielded unrestricted power over the lives of his children. Usually, infants with any kind of defect were drowned in the river Tiber. Romulus, believed to be the founder and first monarch of Rome, restricted the power of family patriarchs. During the centuries preceding the birth of Christ, more and more deaf people were allowed to live and granted certain rights. Under the rule of emperor Augustus (63 BC - 14 AD) deaf people who showed talent were even schooled in fine arts.

In his *Encyclopedia of Natural History* the scientist Pliny the Elder, who perished in the eruption of Vesuvius in Pompei in 79 AD, wrote, "There are no persons born deaf that are not also dumb." (David Wright quotes him in his book, *Deafness, a Personal Account* from 1969.)

Deafness was regarded as the primary condition to which muteness was secondary. Pliny tells of a congenitally deaf man named Quintus Pedius, who had been schooled as a painter. Pedius, who became a prominent painter, is the first deaf man whose name has gone to history. He was the grandson of a Roman consul. For many years, deaf education was available only to the children of wealthy and influential parents. Although deaf peoples´ standing improved, as late as the reign of Emperor Justianus the First (482 - 565 AD) they were still denied the right to take part in public activities. They were not allowed to own property or to draw up a will.

Quintus Pedius

The language of gestures and mime was highly respected by the Romans. There were six thousand professional pantomime artists in Rome who functioned as mediators and interpreters. Rome was regarded as the capital of the world at that time. It was the meeting place for representatives from many different cultures and the pantomime interpreters translated their languages. Emperor Charlemagne (742-814), a wise and mighty ruler, a figure head of unified Christiandom, adhering to a clerical edict, prohibited pantomime. Deaf people, with their gestural language, probably worked as pantomimists.

The Jews

The status of the deaf in Jewish society was better than among the Greeks or Romans though not as advantageous as in ancient Egypt. The Jews offered no privileges to the deaf but allowed them to live.

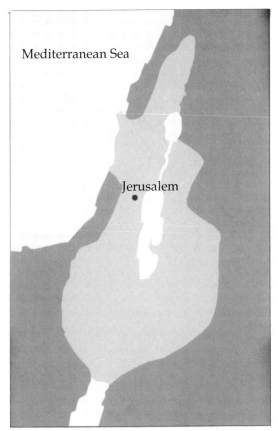

The map shows the "Promised Land" of the Jews from c. 926. The area was divided between Isreal in the north and Judah in the south.

According to the laws of Moses, the crippled were barred from holy places. This applied to the blind, the lame etc. The deaf, however, were allowed into the temple and other shrines. In the book of Leviticus 19:14, the Old Testament reads: "You shall not curse the deaf or put a stumbling block before the blind, but you shall fear your God : I am the Lord."

In the book of Proverbs 31:8 King Solomon even demanded special deference: "Open your mouth for the dumb, for the rights of all who are left desolate."

The episode where a deaf man is brought to Jesus for help gives us proof of the compassion shown the deaf. Jesus said, *"Eph'phatha"* (be opened) and the deaf man could hear and speak (Mark 7:32).

Christianity

Christianity, the interpretation of the life and person of Jesus by the Christian community, arose in a time of religious decline.

Due to peace and improved transpor-

Jesus healing a deaf and dumb youth by the laying on of hands to his ear and lips. From a miniature in an antiphonary in Liberia Piccolomini in Siena by Liberale da Verona (1445-1526, 29).

tation, Christianity could easily reach more people in the Roman Empire. People of various nationalities: Jews, Greeks and Romans, were converted to Christianity.

Along with Christianity came a more charitable attitude among people. With mild benevolence, the deaf were cared for and given food according to the teachings of Christianity.

For the deaf, however, the spiritual situation was just as dark as before, and it remained so for centuries, perhaps mainly due to the fact that Augustine (354 to 430), the foremost scholar and patriarch of the church in the western hemisphere, regarded the ear as the "gate of salvation" (cf. A. F. Nyström, 1907 and O. Österberg, 1925).

He was, then, in almost complete agreement with Aristotle who, 750 years earlier, deemed that all learning must pass through the ear. Augustines pronouncement that the "Deaf and dumb cannot attain faith, for faith stems from the sermon, the spoken word" was interpreted as meaning that the deaf were incapable of salvation.

Romans 10:17, in the revised standard version of 1946 of the New Testament, reads: "So faith comes from what is heard, and what is heard comes by the preaching of Christ."

After having studied the writings of Augustine in the original Latin at the University of Lund, Christer Degsell (1981) arrived at a different view of his opinions on the spiritual state of the deaf. The writings of Augustine fill fifteen volumes in which he covers virtually everything that has to do with the life of mankind. They are a source from which to under-

stand the views of the church on handicap and the handicapped.

Deafness is an obstacle to comprehension of the spoken word

On the subject of original sin, Augustine writes, "Why is it that the innocent are sometimes born blind, sometimes deaf?"

The latter handicap is an obstacle to faith. Augustine attempts to explain why innocent people, even newborn babies who have done no evil, can fall victim to misfortune and handicap. To think that Augustine believed the deaf could not attain salvation is to misunderstand his teachings. He merely held that deafness makes it more difficult to receive the

Saint Augustine

Cui DEVS egregias indulsit ab æthere dotes
Non ego donatum cælitus esse neant?

word, the sermon. It is difficult for the deaf to comprehend spoken words.

Sign language - the visible word

Augustine regards gestures and signs made with the hands as visible words. He refers to them by the Latin term, *verba visibila*, regarding this as a way for those who cannot hear to receive Christian teachings and attain faith.

To Augustine deafness is not an insurmountable obstacle to salvation. The obstacle is the fact that the spoken word cannot reach the deaf. The word must be made visible.

To him it was of no importance if a person was handicapped or not; the important point was the question of sin and absolution, how mankind is to be saved. It is the will of God that all mankind be saved and learn the truth.

The church father Augustine realized over 1550 years ago that the deaf can be addressed with visible words, signs, so that they can come to know the lord of the church, Jesus Christ.

The Koran

Mohammed was born around the year 570 AD in Mecca in Arabia where he lived as a camel driver and caravan guide until he had a series of visions which he interpreted as the call of God to become a prophet to his people, the Arabs.

The holy scripture of Islam is the Koran, believed to have been revealed, word for word, to Mohammed by God, partly through the archangel Gabriel.

The deaf and the blind are mentioned in several places in the Koran , but only briefly. One instance is this passage:

> **Ar-room**
> *52. For verily thou canst not make the dead to hear and thou canst not make the deaf to hear the call, when they withdraw turning their backs.*
> *53. Nor canst thou lead the blind out of their straying. Thou canst not make hear any but those who believe in Our signs for they are resigned (to Our will, i.e. Muslims).*

The Koran must be interpreted literally: the deaf are totally incurable and nothing can be done about them.

The Venerable Bede, 672-735, England

The Venerable Bede was an English munk who wrote *De Temporum Ratione* (Farrar) or *De Computo vel Loquela Digitorum* (von der Lieth). This book contains the world´s oldest picture of Roman numerals displayed with the fingers. In his foreword, Bede wrote that the finger positions can represent letters. This hand-alphabet was first intended to be used as a secret language for the hearing, as in the case of the hand-language of diamond dealers in Amsterdam.

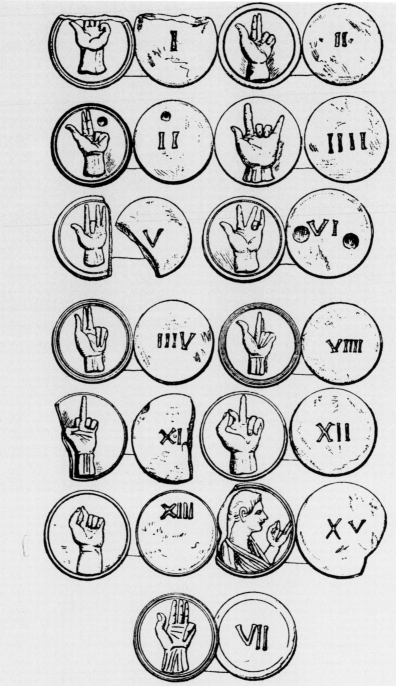

The world´s oldest picture of Roman numerals displayed on the fingers. From the Venerable Bede´s De Computo vel Loquela Digitorum, England, 672 - 735.

The First Teacher of the Deaf

In his *History of the English Church and People*, the Venerable Bede describes the following:

Around the year 700 AD St. John of Beverley was archbishop of York, England. He was the first person known to have taught the deaf. He was the first to reject Aristotle´s and Augustine´s mistaken theory that the deaf are ineducable.

The story goes that each week there came a poor, slovenly, deaf youth to the archbishop´s door to beg for alms. The archbishop´s gift brought tears of gratitude to the eyes of the deaf boy. The archbishop noticed that the lad had noble feelings and an intelligent face. He decided to try to teach the boy to talk.

According to this half-legendary story from the murky middle ages, St. John taught the boy to say "a", "b" etc. By the end of one day, the deaf boy had learned to say syllables, words and sentences! That sounds like a cross between teaching and healing, but some people regard St. John of Beverley as the first teacher of the deaf. He died in 721.

The Turks

The history of Turkey is not known until around the year 1280. We know very little about what standing the deaf had in Turkey at this time. Their fate was determined by the whim of the sultan. Deaf people are believed to have been harem servants and deaf pantomimists are thought to have entertained the sultan.

The Legal Standing of the Deaf

The judicial history of deafness begins with Judaic law. The Talmud distinguishes between those who are deaf and dumb and those who are only deaf or only dumb. Deaf-mutes were not considered capable of owning property, which meant they did not have the same legal rights as other people. This law was adopted by the Romans who made further distinction between degrees of deafness. Five different categories were eventually listed in the *Justinian Code*.

1. Those born deaf and dumb
2. Those who become deaf and dumb after birth
3. Those born deaf but not dumb
4. Those who have lost their hearing but are not dumb
5. Those who are dumb

Those born deaf and dumb had neither rights nor obligations in Roman society. They could neither own property nor draw up a contract. Deaf people who could speak, on the other hand, had legal rights. They were allowed to own property, marry, and write wills.

These laws and distinctions were retained in most legal codes based on Roman Law.

This meant that a deaf-mute could not inherit land. The land and title went instead to the closest relative. This was a problem for many landed families in Spain during the sixteenth century, where intermarriage and hereditary deafness were common.

From the middle of the sixteenth century on, ever greater efforts were made to educate the deaf. What can be called the history of deaf education has its beginnings in this period.

Deaf education from the sixteenth century until the present day can be divided into three major periods.

The First Phase: Until 1760

In the first phase of the history of deaf education, deaf children of wealthy families were tutored individually. The education and rearing of children was arranged for privately by their families. Tutors of the deaf were usually physicians or priests by profession. The writings of many such tutors indicate that they worked at a very elementary level, the purpose of the lessons being to teach the deaf child to communicate with the hearing people around him.

Instruction was offered only to a few deaf persons, privately and in only a few countries, primarily Spain, Great Britain, Germany, Holland and France. We shall trace the development of deaf education in these countries and get to know some of the tutors.

Rudolph Agricola of Groningen, Holland and Heidelberg, Germany, 1433-85

Toward the end of the fifteenth century, Rudolph Agricola, professor of philosophy at Heidelberg, took an interest in alleviating the lot of the deaf and opening even to them the gates to the realm of knowledge. He taught a deaf-born pupil to communicate through both speech and writing. We have no record of the name of the pupil nor of where this teaching took place. Agricola died in 1485 and in 1538 his book *De Inuentione Dialectica* was published posthumously. The book was received with scepticism. At that time, and particularly before the printing press, virtually all learning was by ear. The deaf were assumed to have no access to intellec-

Rudolph Agricola

RUDOLPH AGRICOLA

Zie hier t afbeeldzel van dien grooten Redenaar
En tweeden Maro, die met zyn vergode smaar
En heerlyk orgelwerk zoo kragtig zig liet hooren.
Dat het van Grunoos stadt klonk tot aan'shemels kooren.

G. Outhof

22

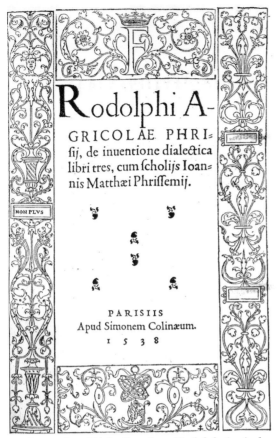

De Inuentione Dialectica, from Rudolph Agricola

Earlier, muteness was regarded as an anatomical defect like deafness and presumed to be medically curable. The first to explain the connection between deafness and muteness was the famous physician and philosopher, Girolamo Cardano i Pavia, Italy. He contributed greatly to our understanding of the problems of the deaf. His eldest son was deaf in one ear and he himself had a stammer; hence his interest in the problems of the deaf. Cardanus reasoned that the lack of a sense does not necessarily mean inferior intelligence; that the deaf are educable and that, with the help of writing, they could develop intellectually. His basic thesis was that "Writing is associated with speech and speech with thought; but written characters and ideas

tual instruction. Because of the poor communications and transportation of the time, word of Agricola´s work did not get around and he had no immediate followers. No new developments occurred in the field of deaf education until more than a half a century later.

Girolamo Cardano, 1501-76, Italy

At the beginning of the sixteenth century, deafness and the muteness it caused were no longer regarded as obstacles to influence on the intellect.

Girolamo Cardano, called "Hieronymus Cardanus" in Latin

may be connected without the intervention of actual sounds."

These ideas were revolutionary in the sixteenth century. Deaf education had become theoretically possible. Unfortunately, Cardanus never put his theories into practice. There is no record of his having taught deaf pupils. He put forth his ideas in a work entitled *Paralipomenon*.

Juan Fernandez Navarrete, Deaf Painter, 1526-79, Spain

We know of several deaf painters. One of the most famous of them was Juan Fernandez Navarrete. He was born in Spain around 1526, to noble parents and lost his hearing at the age of three.

Drawing became Navarrete´s medium of expression for his thoughts and desires. He showed great talent and his father arranged formal training for him.

Navarrete´s painting teacher was the munk, Francisco Vicente from the monastery L'Etoile in Estella. Navarrete was called *El Mudo* (the mute) and sent to Italy to study with Tizian.

He was later summoned to Madrid where he became court painter to King Philip the Second. El Mudo travelled extensively and became very famous. Because of his magnificent coloration, he was known as "the Spanish Tizian". His paintings, which came to be highly valued, were bold depictions of strong emotion. Aside from many religious motifs, he painted protraits of the king and other distinguished members of the court. His paintings are preserved in Escorial.

El Mudo was known to communicate through signs, reading and writing and playing cards. He was well versed in religious and secular history, and also in mythology. He expressed himself with signs which those who conversed with him found impressively clear.

Upon the death of El Mudo in Toledo in 1579, Lope de Vega wrote of him that, although mute himself, he never painted a mute face. In prose translation, Lope de Vega´s epitaph for El Mudo reads,

Heaven denied me speech, that by my understanding I might give greater feeling to the things which I painted; and such great life did I give them with my skillful pencil, that as I could not speak I made them speak for me. (Wright, 1969. p. 134)

> *Finger-spelling was invented in settings where speech was either prohibited or inhibited. To invent a system of finger-spelling one had to be able to spell. Literacy was, however, not wide-spread during the renaissance. Only the well educated could invent systems of finger-spelling.*

Giovanni Battista della Porta, 1535-c.1610, Italy

Giovanni Battista della Porta devised a primitive hand alphabet consisting of pointing to different parts of the body, for example: the ear, *Auris*, for A; the beard, *Barda*, for B; the head, *Caput*, for C, a tooth, *Dentes*, for D. This system is described in *De Furtivis Literarum Notis*, printed in

24

Naples in 1563. Battista´s system was referred to repeatedly by theoreticians of his time, but never applied in teaching the deaf.

Cosmas Rosselius, the 1570s, Italy

In the monasteries speech was frowned upon. The munks devised silent, discreet forms of communication, using many different types of finger-spelling. Cosmas Rosselius from Florence was a Franciscan

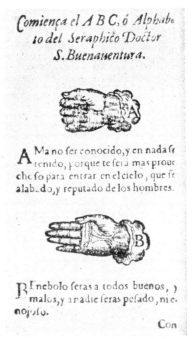

A page from de Yebra´s Refugium Informorum

The oldest known illustration of a one-hand alphabet. Wood cut in the Thesaurus Artificiosae Memoriae by Cosmas Rosselius, printed in Venice in 1579.

priest who died sometime between 1575 and 1578. In 1579 his work, *Thesaurus Artificiosae Memoriae* (A Glossary of Signs), was published posthumously in Venice. This book contains five plates showing three different one-hand alphabets and fifty-two configurations of the fingers. All three alphabets clearly show that an effort has been made to mirror written characters. For most letters, three alternatives are presented, but only two for the letters S, T and V and none for J,K,R,U,W,Y or Z. Rosselius, too, illustrated a system of pointing to places on the human body. The munks, reluctant to put such a system to use, stuck to finger-spelling.

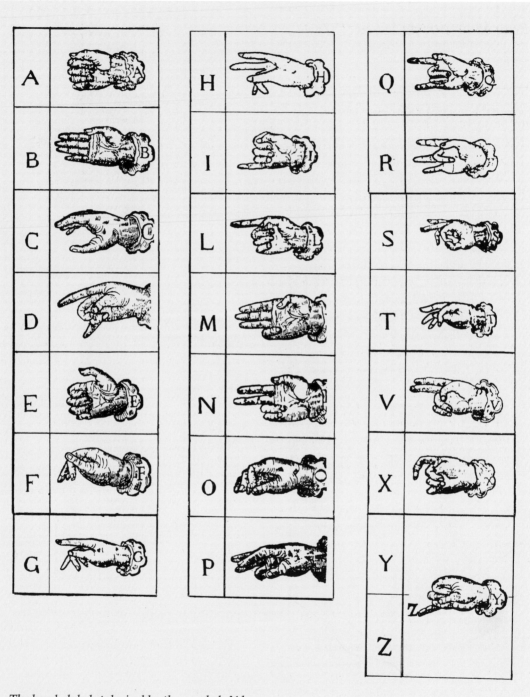

The hand alphabet devised by the munk de Yebra.

Fray Melchior de Yebra, 1526-86, Spain

In southern European countries, various systems of finger-spelling have been in use for hundreds of years. In monasteries, finger-spelling was used as early as the thirteenth century.

Fray Melchior de Yebra was a munk of the Franciscan order in Madrid. In the year 1593 his little book entitled *Refugium Informorum, por el Padre Fray Melchior de Yebra* was posthumously published. This book was a kind of guide to confession containing six pages of illustrations of hand positions with which a dying person no longer able to speak could make his last confession.

This system could also be used to communicate with deaf people who had learned it.

Like Rosselius´ system of fingerspelling, Yebra´s hand alphabet shows many similarities to written letters. Some of the signs do not, however, correspond to written letters at all; for instance "A", which is signed with a closed hand.

Yebra´s finger-spelling system can also be found in the oldest preserved manual for deaf education, written in 1620 by Juan Pablo Bonet.

Pedro Ponce de León, c.1520-84, Spain

Pedro Ponce de León was born in Valladolid in the province of León around the year 1520. He was a graduate of the Univer-

Pedro Ponce de León

sity of Salamanca. At the age of thirty, he became a munk in the Benedictine monastery San Salvador in Ona near Burgos, León.

Apparently, Ponce´s interest in the deaf was the result of a personal meeting. Gaspard Burgos was a deaf man who wanted to become a munk at San Salvador. Due to his deafness this was, however, out of the question; being unable to speak, he could not make his confession. Ponce took an interest in Burgos and taught him to write and speak. As no exact record of this incident has survived, we can only guess that this deaf youth was the son of some noble Spanish house.

At this time, Spain was at the height of its wealth and power. Enormous riches impounded from South and Central America were now in the hands of comparatively few families of Spanish nobility. Class differences were great in Spanish society of that period;

intermarriage was a commonplace thing, and sometimes the heirs to estates were born deaf.

According to Roman law, deaf mutes could not inherit fortunes. They were not allowed to own property or to write wills. On the other hand, those who were only deaf and not mute did have legal rights. Deaf people who could speak were entitled own and will property. The moneyed classes in Spain, eager to educate their deaf offspring, opposed the Inquisition conducted by the Catholic church.

Ponce´s incentive to tutor the deaf was primarily religious. Around 1570, he tutored four deaf children: two sons and a daughter of the field marshal of Castille, the sons being Don Francisco and Don Pedro de Velasco, and Gaspar de Burrea, son of governor Gaspar de Burgos of Aragon.

Ponce´s goal was to teach his charges to speak, but they were not trained in lipreading. He would point at labeled objects and have his pupils pronounce the names of them. They were taught to read, write and speak. After this schooling, they were able to make spoken confession, recite prayers and assist at mass. A hand-written document from this period, the oldest record of deaf education in Spain, describes the legal rights and status Francisco de Velascos acquired by learning to speak.

Ponce communicated with his pupils in writing and by finger-spelling. All notes in his own hand were lost in a fire in the monastery library at San Salvador. We know of his methods through documentation left by his students. There are also descriptions of Ponce by two of his contemporaries: Ambrosio de Morales, a Spanish historian, and Franciscus Valesius, the personal physician to Philip the Second.

Ponce was among the first to realize that muteness as a rule is the result of the inability to hear and therefore not curable by surgery. To him muteness was a consequence of deafness. Ponce, who died in 1584, was called the father of deaf education. On his tombstone is carved: "Pedro Ponce educated the deaf and dumb though Aristotle declared it impossible."

Juan Pablo Bonet, 1579-1629, Spain

After the death of Ponce de León, deaf education was carried on by Juan Pablo Bonet and Emanuel Ramirez de Carrión.

Juan Pablo Bonet

28

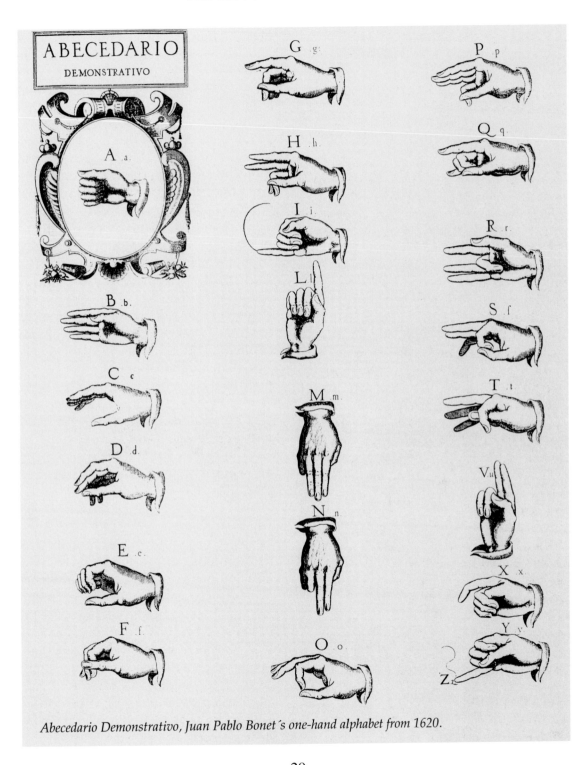

Abecedario Demonstrativo, Juan Pablo Bonet´s one-hand alphabet from 1620.

Bonet, originally a soldier and merchant, became secretary to the Constable of Castille, a great-nephew of Ponce de

The title page of Reduction de las Letras, y Arte para Enseñar a Hablar a los Mudos *by Juan Pablo Bonet, Madrid, 1620. This was the first scientific treatise on deaf education. The inscripton on the ribbon wound around the pillars is illustrated to the left by birds liberated from their cage and to the right by a padlock on the tongue of a deaf-mute being unlocked with a writing quill as a key. At the top in the middle is the coat of arms of the kings of Spain, beneath that, the de Velasco family coat of arms, and at the bottom, probably that of the Bonet family.*

León´s students. The Field Marshal´s younger brother, Luis de Velasco, the marquis of Fresno, was deaf like his great-uncles. Hereditary deafness was common in these families.

Bonet published the book *The Simplification of the Letters of the Alphabet and the Art of Teaching Deaf Mutes to Speak* in 1620 in Madrid while functioning as courtier to Philip the Third of Spain. It is the oldest preserved textbook on deaf education.

In teaching the deaf, Ponce and Bonet adopted the finger-spelling created by munks for silent communication. Bonet´s dissertation on deaf education is illustrated with the engraving, *Abecedario Demonstrativo*, a one-hand alphabet of which an almost exact replica is still in use in America. (cf. fig. on page 29).

The hand alphabet used by Ponce and Bonet was published in Rosselius´s *Artificiosae Memoriae* (Venice 1579) forty-one years before Bonet´s book. Bonet must have been familiar with Yebra´s booklet *Refugium Informorum*, too, because Bonet´s and Yebra´s systems are almost exactly identical.

Bonet´s book consists of two parts. The first, *Reduction de las Letras* (The Simplification of Letters of the Alphabet) is about sounding out words and is the first known text on phonetics. It was not until the nineteenth century that phonetics, the study of speech sounds, became an established scientific field. In this first part of his book, Bonet attempts to show similarities between the articulation of sounds and the forms of letters. The second part is a detailed description of a method of teaching speech and language to the deaf Written words and finger-spelling were used in teaching. Bonet insisted that everyone around the deaf students either finger-spell or write rather than sign to them. The students were required to respond orally. Lipreading was practiced only with simultaneous finger-spelling.

To teach speech, Bonet demonstrated the positions of the tongue using an artificial one made of leather. The students were taught the letters of the alphabet first, then their finger-spelled equivalents and, after that, language sounds. They were then to learn to read. Bonet's method later came to be called the Spanish method.

In Bonet's times, it was hard to get anything published, particularly in the ultra-Catholic country of Spain, where anything innovative was banned by the Inquisition. Before it was allowed to be published, Bonet's book had to be approved by the officials of both Castille and Aragon. The manuscript was subject to perusal by the ecclesiastical censors, Padre Manuel Mola at a Dominican monastery in Madrid and Padre Antonio Perez at a Benedictine monastery in the same city. Both of these priests were in the service of the Castillian government.

In 1620, the book was licensed by the royal court with various stipulations, for example that the book should be in print for ten years and printing errors corrected, have a set price of 270 maravedis (approximately fifty cents or thirty pence): a rather high price at that time. The book must undergo further censorship under the supervision of Friar Miguel Betram of the Montesa Order, prior of the San Juan de Borriana monastery and priest to the court of his majesty the King of Aragon, in whose name the licence for publication was issued in 1620.

A photgraphic facsimile of Bonet's book from 1620 was printed in Madrid as recently as 1929.

Emanuel Ramirez de Carrión, 1579-1652, Spain

At the time when Bonet's book came out in 1620, Emanuel Ramirez de Carrión was tutoring the deaf Spaniard, Marquis Prisgo. Carrión worked as a secretary and a teacher. He describes his teaching method in the book, *Maravillas de Naturaleza Enque se Contienen dos Mil Secretos de Cosas*

Maravillas de Naturaleza

31

Naturales ("The Marvels of Nature") published in Madrid in the year 1629. His teaching methods were influenced by midieval pracitce and by the Inquisition in an ultra-Catholic country. Before each lesson, the student was given an appropriate laxative whereupon he was to imbibe a potion containing sneezing powder, the last dose accompanied by various herbal juices. Then an area the size of a hand was shaved on the top of the student´s head in the style of the tonsure of Catholic munks. Every evening, a concoction of alcohol, saltpeter, bitter almonds and oil was rubbed into this bare spot. Each morning the student must comb the top of his head with an ebony comb and then eat a paste of mastic, amber, musk and licorice root. The student must then wash his face and dry his nose and ears very carefully. After that, Carrión pronounced the separate letters of the alphabet first, then syllables and finally the

Kenelm Digby

names of familiar objects over the top of the student´s head. The student repeated these after the teacher and in a short time he acquired great skill in the art of speech. The Enbecome Charles the First) spoke to Carrión´s student while on a visit to Spain in 1622. The deaf student expressed himself distinctly and clearly although with monotonous intonation according to Digby´s account in his *Treatise on the Nature of Bodies* of the year 1644 (referred to by Keller under the title of *Demonstratio Immortalitatis Animae*).

Diego Ramirez de Carrión, Spain

The son of Emanuel Ramirez de Carrión, Diego Ramirez de Carrión used his father´s teaching methods. One of his students was Sister Josefa Gevsmán, a Franciscan nun in the convent of Medina Sidonia. Diego Ramirez de Carrión was awarded a state pension for his accomplishments in the field of deaf education. His home was in Escolapios, Spain.

Francis Mercurius van Helmont, 1618-99, Belgium

Baron Francis van Helmont was a Belgian occultist and chemist who spent most of his life in Sulzbach, Germany. In the year 1667 he published the book, *Kurzer Entwurf des eigentlichen Natur-Alphabets der Heiligen Sprache: Nach dessen Anleitung Man auch Taubgeborene verstehend und redend machen kann* (A Short Sketch of the True Natural Alphabet of the Holy Language: With the Aid of Which even Those Born

Deaf can be Made to Understand and Speak).

Helmont believed that Hebrew would be the easiest language for the deaf to learn and therefore the best one to use for their education. In his book, he asserts that the letters of the Hebrew alphabet are illustrations of the positions of the vocal organs when each sound is pronounced. The book contains thirty-six illustrations of speech sounds.

Helmont writes that the deaf can lipread

This illustration from Helmont´s Natural Alphabet shows a man using a compass to measure the opening of his mouth as he pronounces a vowel in the mirror. It is one of the earliest representations of lipreading.

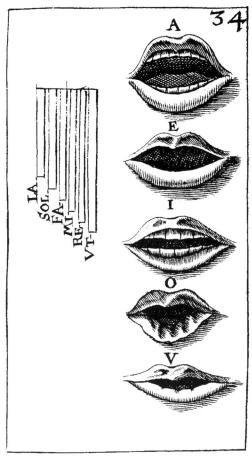

The positions of the lips when pronouncing "a", "e", long "e", "o" and "u" (printed as "v" in early texts), from Helmont´s Natural Alphabet.

if one speaks slowly to them. In three weeks he taught a deaf person to speak. The deaf man could lipread and answer questions orally.

Johan Konrad Amman, 1669-1724, Switzerland and Holland

Johan Konrad Amman was born in the Swiss town of Schaffhausen in 1669. His father was a municipal physician and he himself received a degree in medicine. He

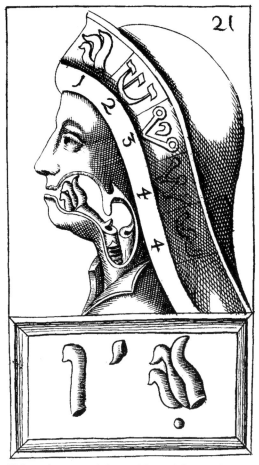

Hebrew letters and the positions of the speech organs. from Helmont´s Natural Alphabet.

specialized in the study of the vocal organs and speech sounds.

As a young man, Amman moved to the Netherlands where he practiced Medicine in Amsterdam and Haarlem. A wealthy burgher came to his surgery seeking help for his deaf and dumb daughter, Esther Collard. She was given speech training at Amman´s country estate near Leyden. In lieu of medical treatment for muteness, Amman taught speech to his deaf and dumb patients. He taught them voiced and unvoiced speech sounds and the pro-

per positioning of the vocal organs. They also practiced lipreading.

Amman recorded his experience in two books, which were to have a great influence on subsequent deaf education in the rest of Europe. The first, *Surdus Loquens* (The Talking Deaf Man) was published in 1692 and the second, *Dissertatio de Loquela* (Dissertation on Language) in the year 1700. Amman´s two books emphasized the importance of speech and became the basis of what was later called the German method, the oral method or speech method of deaf education. Amman

A portrait of Johan Konrad Amman by Johann Friedrich Wettstein (1659-1744), Basel. The original was lost in the bombing of the city of Schaffhausen in 1944.

THE
Talking Deaf Man:
OR, A
Method Propofed,

Whereby he who is Born

DEAF,

May Learn to

SPEAK.

By the Studious Invention and
Induftry of *John Conrade
Amman*, an *Helvetian* of
Shafhuis, Dr. of Phyfick.

Imprinted at *Amfterdam*, by *Henry
Weftein*, 1692. And now done
out of Latin into Englifh, by
D. F. M. D. 1693.

London, Printed for **Tho. Howkins**,
in *George-yard, Lumbard ftreet*, 1694.

Price bound **One Shilling.**

*The Talking Deaf Man, an English translation of
Amman´s book from 1694.*

John Bulwer, 1614-84, England

England was the cradle of deaf education.
It was here that the "first teacher of the
deaf", John de Beverley, lived around 700.
The first after him to take an interest in
educating the deaf in England was John
Bulwer, physician and anthropologist. He
published three works: *Chirologia or the
Natural Language of the Hand* in 1644, *Chironomia* (a set of plates of manual gestures) in 1648 and *Philocophus or the Deaf and
Dumb Man´s Friend* the same year.

Bulwer was of the opinion that the deaf

John Bulwer in 1653

was regarded as the father of the speech
method — the Amman method. He explained that the reason the deaf, normally
equipped with vocal organs, do not speak
is that they cannot hear. They can, however, learn to speak. Amman made it his
job to teach speech to the deaf. His books,
originally in Latin, were translated into
many languages and published in many
editions, finding readers all over Europe.
Until his death in 1724, Amman went on
teaching speech to the deaf.

Bulwer´s Chirologia from 1644 includes signs for emotions and states of mind.

A. I implore
B. I request
C. I lament
D. I admire
E. I applaud
F. I dislike
G. I reject
H. I dispair
I. I relax
K. I am sad
L. I am innocenrt
M. I prefer
N. I refrain
O. I protect
P. I triumph
Q. Silence, please
R. I swear
S. I assure you
T. I elect
V. I dismiss
W. I invite
X. I dismiss
    (an employee)
Y. I threaten
Z. I beg

deer for hearing, a dog for smell and a monkey for taste. The symbols on the shields opposite these are blotted out and replaced by others.

should first learn to write and then speak which would then make learning to lipread easier. To him, it was perfectly acceptable for the deaf to gesticulate when communicating, but they should also be able to lipread as well as speak and write intelligibly.

Bulwer´s books interested others in deaf education, but we have no historical

The engraved title page of John Bulwer´s Philocophus or the Deaf and Dumb Man´s Friend *(London 1648), an illustration of how the senses we have can substitute senses we lack. In the lower lefthand corner, the sound from a* viola de gamba *is conducted through the teeth of a deaf man. On the table in the lower righthand corner lie a picture, a censer and a bowl of fruit, each connected by a dotted line to the sensory organ used to compensate a missing sense. On the four heads at the bottom of the picture an eye and a tongue are in the place of the nose, eyes in the ears and an ear in place of an eye. The main senses are illustrated allegorically on the shields held by the four figures in teh upper lefthand corner: an eagle for sight, a*

Some illustrations of signs from Bulwer´s Chirologia, *London 1644.*

evidence of his ever having put his theories into practice.

George Dalgarno, 1626-87, England

George Dalgarno was born around the year 1626 in Aberdeen, Scotland. He was the headmaster of a school in Oxford, England where he also worked as a teacher. He was one of the many seventeenth century intellectuals who pondered on the nature of language.

In 1680 his *Didascalocophus or the Deaf and Dumb mans Tutor* was published with an entirely new system of spelling with the hands. To learn it, one wears a glove, painted with the letters of the alphabet; with the other hand, one points to the place where each letter of a word is painted. Once the position of each letter is memorized, spelling can be done without the glove.

Dalgarno´s system has been used intermittently until the present day in the United States and other countries. One of the educators of the deaf to revive it in the nineteenth century was Alexander Graham Bell.

Dalgarno´s most significant contribution to deaf education, though, was incorporating into it the innovations of the great reformer of education, Comenius. Comenius understood that we learn from what we see around us, rather than by mindlessly repeating the phrases dictated to us by a teacher as was the method of instruction in the middle ages. We must be taught words as we are learning about the nature of things. Comenius was the first to design a book of educational charts for children.

Dalgarno continued the work Comenius had begun, believing that deaf children learn best through play; not by drilling grammar or having every word and syllable

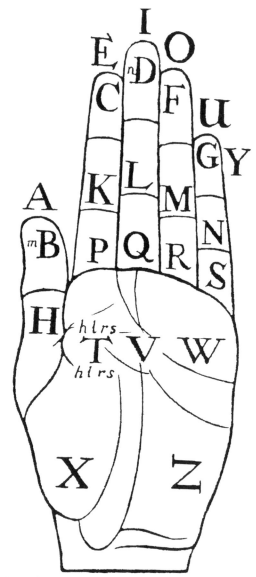

A woodcut from George Dalgarno´s Didascalocophus or the Deaf and Dumb mans Tutor

38

pedantically corrected. Most important is that the deaf student truly understands what he learns.

John Wallis, 1616-1703, England

John Wallis was professor of geometry at Oxford for more than half a century. During the English civil war he used his knowledge of mathematics to decode messages. Wallis was also interested in language. In 1653 he wrote *Tractatus Physicus de Loquela*, an English grammar book including a chapter on phonetics.

In the year 1661, Wallis started to tutor two deaf aristocrats, one of whom was Daniel Whaley from Northampton who had lost his hearing at he age of five. After one year of tutoring and having perused a large portion of the Bible, the deaf students could understand written texts and express themselves intelligibly in writing. They could even read Latin!

In May of 1662, Danial Whaley was presented at a London scientific society and at the royal palace. He was asked to read a text just handed to him. His speech was toneless, but clear enough to understand.

The written word was the medium of most of Wallis´ instruction. He is considered the father of the writing method of deaf education. Sometimes finger-spelling was used to save time. Speech and lipreading were also used in his classes. He considered gestural language as important as speech.

William Holder, 1615-97, England

William Holder was a pastor in Oxfordshire and headmaster of a school in Bretchington, England. His book, *Elements of Speech*, published in London in 1669, includes an "Appendix Concerning Persons Deaf and Dumb". The volume was translated into Latin and then German (under the title, *Anfangsgründe der Sprache*). Holder describes tutoring Alexander Popham, a deaf boy related to the Earl of Oxford. An inventive man, Holder used a strip of leather to illustrate tongue movements in articulation. Popham, however, forgot how to talk after his schooling with Holder and his mother took him to Wallis, whose teaching methods had a better effect. Holder was not happy about losing a student to Wallis.

Wallis considered himself a pioneer of deaf education. He found fault in Holder´s

John Wallis, an engraving from 1765

A two-hand alphabet was proposed by John Wallis in 1652.

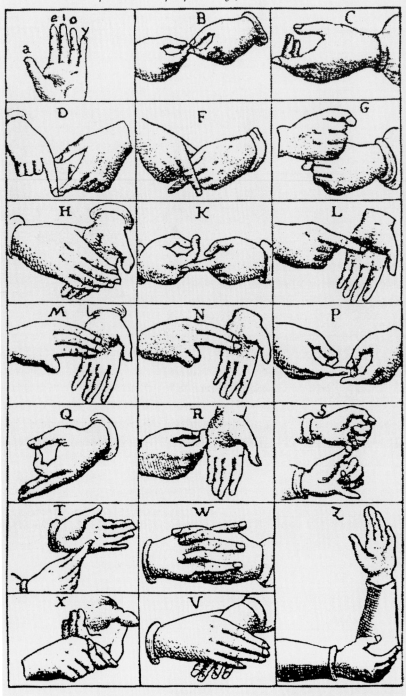

Wallis´s two-hand alphabet is pictured in the novel, The History of the Life and Adventures of Mr. Duncan Campbell *by Daniel Defoe (London 1720). This hand alphabet is similar to the one used in Great Britain today and to the one used in Norway until 1970.*

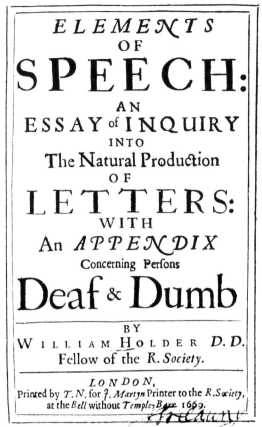

Elements of Speech, from Holder

Henry Baker

speech teaching and also criticized him for not devoting more time to teaching his student to write. This resulted in a heated and longdrawn public spat between the two learned gentlemen. This academic dispute had the positive effect of calling more puplic attention to the issue of deaf education.

Henry Baker, 1698-1774, England

As a young man, Henry Baker visited relatives in Enfield. One of them was an eight year-old deaf girl and Baker was confident that he could teach her language and speech.

Around this time (1720), Daniel Defoe´s book *The History of the Life and Adventures of Mr. Duncan Campbell* had come out. Campbell was deaf, had been schooled by the methods of Wallis, but had never learned to speak. The public was more interested in his supposed clairvoyant and fortune-telling talents than in his deafness. Most of the book is about parapsychology, but the first chapters do describe the life situation of a deaf person and include a description of Wallis´ method.

Baker was inspired by this book when he set out to tutor his first student, Jane Forster of Enfield. The lessons were very successful and Baker could charge high fees and make his living as a teacher of the deaf.

He wanted his methods to be kept a

Duncan Campbell

Joakim Pascha

secret and made his students promise not to divulge them. He also chose his students carefully to guard against the bad publicity of a failure.

Joakim Pascha, 1527-78, Germany

At the end of the fifteenth century, Agricola, a professor in Heidelberg tutored a deaf student. There is no record of the name of this student, the place where the tutoring took place or the methods used.

The next known instance of the tutoring of deaf pupils in Germany is from approximately one hundred years later when Joakim Pascha, ecclesiastical minister to the Elector Joakim II of Brandenburg, instructed the Elector's deaf daughter, Elisabeth in religion using pictures.

Wilhelm Kerger, early Eighteenth Century, Germany

It was not until the beginning of the eighteenth century that deaf education per se was established in Germany. In 1704, the Schlesian doctor, Wilhelm Kerger wrote his views on deaf education in a Latin epistle entitled *Littera ad Ettmullerum de Cura Surdorum Mutorumque*. He was convinced that deaf people with normal intelligence and good eyesight could learn to read and write. Furthermore, if given enough training, they could learn to speak and lipread. During his lessons he used writing, speech and gestures, but no finger-spelling. His pupils learned reading, writing, speech and lipreading. He advocated mandatory education for the deaf and wanted to devise an international gestural language.

Georg Raphel. 1673-1740, Germany

General interest in deaf education increased from the beginning of the eighteenth century. Several pamphlets on the medical aspects of deafness and various methods of teaching the deaf were now on the market.

More and more people took an interest

Georg Raphel

in deaf education. The most outstanding of these were Raphel, Lasius and Arnoldi. These three men have also published descriptions of their teaching methods. Georg Raphel was a superintendent in Lüneberg and the father of six children, three of whom were deaf girls. He studied the methods of Amman, but for his own daughters he used an ABC-book, teaching them to read by sounding out each letter. Raphel described these lessons in his book, *Die Kunst, Taube und Stumme reden zu Lehren* (The Art of Teaching the Deaf and Dumb to Speak) from 1718. He started with vowel sounds, then added konsonants: "ab, eb, ib, ba, be, bi, ban, bon, bin, osv." After his daughters had learned to read the ABC-book they went on to other books and also learned to write. When they had learned to speak, they mastered more and more difficult words: first the names of objects and, later, words for abstract concepts.

Speech and lipreading were used in communication. The eldest daughter spoke and lipread so well that one could hardly tell she was deaf. Raphel also prepared his daughters for confirmation.

Otto Lasius, Eighteenth Century, Germany

In 1772, the superintendent Otto Lasius started tutoring his deaf relative, Fräulein von Meding. He described how he went about it in his book, *Ausführliche Nachricht von der Geschehenen Unterweisung der taub und stumm geborenen Fräulein von Meding* (A Thorough Report of the Education of Fräulein von Meding, Born Deaf and

Die Gottesfurcht befahl ein Contrefait Zu machen,
Aus dessen Minen nichts als Lieb und Demuth lachen
Die Pallas gab den Grund, die Svada farben her
Und also fragte man, Weß dieses Bildniß Wär!
Die Warheit schrieb dazu, den feinden Zum Verdruß:
Es ist, ihr Kenet ihn Wohl, He. Doctor Lasius.

krakowsky fe: Wrac: J.G.O.R

Dumb) published in Leipzig in the year 1775.

First, Lasius learned the deaf girl´s own sign language, to be able to communicate with her. He then taught her to write and, using Amman´s and Raphel´s method, attempted to teach her speech. When the girl´s parents complained that they found the sound of her voice offensive, Lasius reverted to a method similar to the one used in England by Wallis, emphasizing writing, using fewer hand signs and less finger-spelling. He wanted his pupil to be able to express her own thoughts in writing. Instead of a grammar book, he utilized every day objects and experiences in his lessons, taking every opportunity to teach the girl names of, and facts about, the objects she encountered. She learned the proper phrases for time and place; everything was written down.

Lasius moved from the concrete to the abstract; from the simple to the complex. Fräulein von Meding was taught all concepts and their opposites. He explained them to her using pictures, gestures, facial expressions and writing.

He required the fräulein only to learn the bare necessities of grammar. The deaf girl attained a level of literacy sufficient for reading letters and other easy texts and writing simple stories. She learned arithmetic and geography. Lasius taught her religion, starting with the basics and moving on to more comprehensive aspects.

Johan Ludvig Ferdinand Arnoldi, 1737-83, Germany

Johan Ludvig Ferdinand Arnoldi was born in 1737. After completing his studies, he was employed in the home of a major-general whose son was deaf. He became the boy´s tutor and attempted at first to teach him to speak using what was called Büchner rods, a kind of long hearing tube. This method proving unsuccessful, Arnoldi switched to Amman´s method which gave better results.

Some time later Arnoldi became rector of a parish, but went on teaching the deaf. This instruction was intended to prepare deaf pupils for confirmation. Arnoldi employed the methods of Amman and

Wallis, keeping a journal of his work.

He started speech training in the forth or fifth year. Grammar was systematically drilled and 150 charts of biblical episodes were used for religious instruction. Visual aids were important. The students and their teacher went on many an excursion in the town and out into the country. From a single such outing the children learned more than from days of classroom work.

Arnoldi stressed understanding more than memorization. In a short time his students learned to speak and write.1 Pictures played a vital, and indispensible role in his teaching. Arnoldi described his methodology in several pamphlets, one of which was entitled *Praktische Unterweisung, taubstumme Personen reden und schreiben zu lehren* (A Practical Instruction for Teaching the Deaf and Dumb to Speak and Write, Giessen 1777). Arnoldi died in 1783.

Jacob Rodriguez Péreira

Spanish-Portugese Jew living in exile in France.

He was born in 1715 in the region of Extremadura, near the Portugese border

Jacob Rodríguez Péreira, 1715-80, France

France lagged behind other European countries in the area of deaf education. There is historical evidence of instances of deaf education in France at the end of seventeenth and beginning of the eighteenth centuries, but it tells us nothing of the methods used, the results achieved or the teachers´ identity.

It was not until the middle of the eighteenth century that the first widely known instance of deaf education occurs in France. The first teacher of the deaf we know of was Jacob Rodríguez Péreira, a

The Péreira Medal of Honor

At the First Congress of Teachers of the Deaf in Paris in 1878, the Péreira Medal of Honor was awarded to Ossian Edmund Borg of the Manilla School for the Deaf in Stockholm. The inscription along the edge of the Medalion reads, "There shall no longer be the deaf and dumb, but deaf people who can speak."

in western Spain. He studied at the university of Paris and in 1735, started tutoring his deaf sister using Bonet´s methods. He first became inspired to teach the deaf when he read of Ponce´s book on pedagogics.

Because Jews were persecuted on the Iberian peninsula, Péreira moved to

France, establishing a business in Bordeaux in the year 1741. France became his permanent home.

Péreira made teaching the deaf his profession and in 1744 he took on as a pupil thirteen year-old Aron Beaumarin, a member of the aristocracy in La Rochelle. Péreira won such acclaim as a teacher that his work was brought to the attention of Louis XV by the French Academy of Sciences.

A personal audience with Louis XV was later arranged for Péreira by the Duke de Chaulmes, whose deaf godson, Saboureaux de Fontenay, became Péreira´s most famous pupil. The youth learned to speak quite distinctly and also to write. His teacher, however, honestly admitted that Fonteney´s deafness was of the "second degree".

In 1751, de Fonteney was presented before the Academy of Sciences. His elocution greatly impressed Louis XV. Péreira was granted an annuity of eight hundred livres.

Péreira´s success with his students was widely acclaimed. People thought it was a miracle. His name and reputation spread rapidly to all of Europe. Fired by encouragement from many quarters, Péreira went on teaching and achieving success.

To secure his livelihood, he preferred to keep his methods to himself. What we do know of them comes from publications of the Academy of Sciences, for instance *Mémoire sur l' Instruction d'un Sourd et Muet, qu'il a Présenté à l'Academie Royale des Sciences* and from a periodical to which Péreira contributed in the year 1747 with the article, *Observation Rémarkable sur Deux Enfants Sourds et Muets de Naissance à qui l'on a Appris à Articuler des Sons.*

Saboureaux de Fontenay does give us some idea of the methods used by Péreira. We know he used gestures and a modified version of Bonet´s one-hand alphabet which he called dactylology.

He concentrated on speech and conversation. As the students became more proficient in speech, gestures and finger-spelling were used less. Péreira was the sole proponent of the the younger Spanish school:

1. Articulation training: a few words were learned in a period of twelve to fifteen months.

2. Language acquisition: Péreira took for granted that the deaf child would learn language the same way a hearing child does.

   a. No underlying phonetic meaning was ascribed to the letters of the Latin alphabet.

   b. Finger-spelling was used.

   c. The hand alphabet (dactylology) consisted of three types of signs:

      1. Signs for each letter
      2. Signs for combinations of letters
      3. Signs for speech sounds
      In all, approximately eighty signs were used.

   d. Finger-spelling was accompanied by speech.

   e. Lipreading was not taught.

47

f. Explanations were given in Gestural language.

Péreira was an extremely skilled edu-cator, teaching in all twelve deaf students with excellent results. He died, a famous and honoured man, in 1780.

Ernaud of Bordeaux, Late Eighteenth Century, France

In the late eighteenth century deaf educators were divided into two camps: those who advocated the Spanish method of teaching and advocates of Amman´s method. Two teachers of the deaf, Péreira on the side of the Spanish method and Ernaud in Bordeaux representing the Amman method, were pitched against each other. This battle reached its peak when Péreira brought Solier, the son of a Swiss merchant and a student of Ernaud´s, before the Academy of Sciences and demanded a declaration that the results Ernaud had achieved with this student were inferior to those of earlier teachers.

Ernaud rejected manual language. Following Amman´s method, he taught his deaf students to speak without using writing. Although his students were said to be highly skilled in articulation and lip-reading, Ernaud was criticized for having neglected the spiritual growth of his pupils.

We cannot know for sure how good a teacher Ernaud actually was. J. Blomkvist writes of him that "He assumed the deaf mutes were only partially deaf and attempted to revive his students´ hearing. He is said, too, to have succeeded in improving the hearing of some of them. The use of a hearing trumpet was apparently to no avail."

Claude Francois Deschamps, France, the 1770s

Besides Péreira and Ernaud, there was a third teacher of the deaf in France, the Abbot Claude Francois Deschamps, who founded a school for the deaf in Orleans in the 1770s. He devoted all his time to teaching the deaf as well as donating his entire fortune to the cause of educating deaf children from the lower classes. In his writings, he points out how the deaf compensate for their lack of hearing by using their eyesight. Using both writing and signs in his classes, he taught his students first speech, then lipreading. Then, he taught them the meanings of words. He combined the oral, manual and Spanish methods. In his classes systematic signs, writing, speech, lipreading and finger-spelling were used.

The First Phase of the History of Deaf Education in Brief

1. This period spanned approximately 200 years, from the beginning of the sixteenth until the late eighteenth century.

2. The education of deaf children was usually arranged by the family.

3. Its purpose was to teach the deaf to communicate with other people orally or in writing.

4. The students were rarely taught lip-reading.
5. The media of instruction were speech, writing, finger-spelling and signs.

6. They started with every day situations and pictures, using sign language sparsely.

7. The methods were largely the same; nonetheless, what differences there were caused teachers to disagree about which of them was best.

8. Because teachers jealously guarded the secrets of their trade, the art of deaf education was often veiled in mystery.

9. Unaware of the work done by others, many teachers of the deaf thought their methods were of their own invention.

10. Many teachers of the deaf were priests or physicians.

11. Of all books on deaf education, those by Johan Konrad Amman were the most influential.

12. Most of what was written about deaf education at this time was either theoretical dissertations or reports of results: there was very little description of actual methods.

The Second Phase: 1760 to 1880. Schools for the Deaf.

The second phase of the history of deaf education began in the late eighteenth century when, unbeknown to each other, three men founded schools for the deaf in three countries. Deaf children were now schooled and brought up in groups; their education having taken a more definite form, based on definite principles. These three teachers of the deaf were Abbé Charles-Michel de l' Épée in France, Samuel Heinicke in Germany and Thomas Braidwood in Britain. Many an educator of the the deaf was to follow in the footsteps of either Abbé de L'Épée or Heinicke.

Thomas Braidwood, 1715-1806, Britain

A graduate of the University of Edinburgh, Thomas Braidwood became the proprietor of a school of mathematics in that city. He became a teacher of the deaf by chance. In the year 1760, he was asked to take on a boy by the name of Charles Sherriff who had lost his hearing at the age of three.

Although he had no experience of teaching the deaf, Braidwood was confident that he would succeed. He studied the works of Bulwer, Wallis and Holder and learned to finger-spell. Encouraged by good results with Sherriff, Braidwood took on two more deaf pupils. In 1766, he advertised for deaf students and could soon establish a school for the deaf which became his livelihood. Its students being the offspring of wealthy parents, the

Plates from Deschamps´s school book of 1779

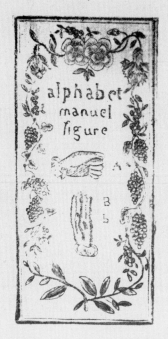

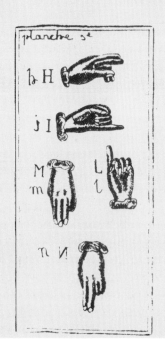

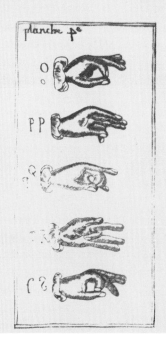

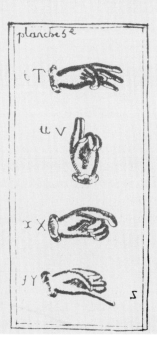

school prospered.

Braidwood patterned his teaching methods mainly on Wallis, using writing and finger-spelling as in the Spanish method. His students learned language by first writing, then articulating the letters of the alphabet moving on to writing and pronouncing whole words.

Some time later, Braidwood wanted to move south and in 1783 The Braidwood Academy was transferred to Hackney in London. Braidwood was accompanied to London by his two nephews, Joseph Watson and John Braidwood (the latter also became his son-in-law). They learned his teaching methods but were sworn to secrecy. When Mr. Braidwood senior died in 1806, Joseph Watson regarded himself as partially released from his oath of secrecy and in 1809 he published *Instruction of the Deaf and Dumb*. There we can read that Braidwood originally based his method on Wallis´s, but modified and improved upon it from his own experience.

Abbé de l'Épée, 1712-89, France

The son of a court architect, Charles-Michel de l'Épée was born on November 24, 1712 at Versailles, the residence of the king of France. Charles-Michel was an excellent student and graduated from the well-known *Collége des Quatre-Nations* at the age of seventeen. Upon leaving school he was faced with the choice of a path in life. His father wanted him to become a lawyer, but, drawn to the priesthood by his devotion to God and mankind, Charles-Michel studied theology.

When the time came for him to be ordai-

Abbé de l´Épée

ned, however, a complication arose. The Catholic Church, wary of what it saw as the depraving influence of Jansenism on young members of the clergy, required all aspirants to the priesthood to sign a written condemnation of the teachings of Jansenism. For ethical reasons, de l'Épée refused to sign such a document and was consequently barred from the priesthood. Instead, complying to the wishes of his family, he studied law and became a lawyer at the age of twenty-one.

Courtroom haggling and law-twisting rhetoric were not, however, the proper element for the gentle, peace-loving de l'Épée. He continued his theological studies in his spare time and did every-thing in his power to persuade the church to reconsider its decision and admit him to the priesthood. His efforts were finally crowned with success. Monseigneur Boussuet, the Bishop of Troyes, impressed by de l'Épée's qualities and moved by his dedication, allowed him to officiate at mass. Finally, in 1738, Charles-Michel was ordained and given the title of Abbé. He was now twenty-six years old.

De l'Épée was to enjoy the position of Abbé for only a few years. Upon the death of the Bishop of Troyes, he was dismissed by the Archbishop of Paris on the grounds that a trained lawyer was not considered appropriate to the priesthood. De l'Épée studied philiosophy and became a doctor in that field. He also learned foreign languages: Spanish, Italian, English. He understood German, which was unusual for a Frenchman.

The Abbé had wealthy parents. When they died, the fortune he inherited brought an annual interest of twelve thousand livres. He became a teacher, for hearing students at first, but later he devoted himself entirely to the education of the deaf.

One summer afternoon in 1760, de l'Épée had some business to attend to in the house across the street from his home on the rue Fossé-Saint-Victor in Paris. He was puzzled when the two adolescent daughters of the house gave no response to his inquiries. When their mother came home, he learned that the girls were deaf and that their tutor, one Father Vanin, had recently passed away.

Much to the delight of their mother, the Abbé immediately offered to take over the girls' education. He had religious motives for offering to tutor the girls and he had no idea how to go about it. In his search for reading matter on the subject he came across the Spaniard Bonet's much talked about book, *The Simplification of the Letters of the Alphabet and the Art of Teaching Deaf Mutes to Speak.* In it he found a copper etching showing *Abecedario*, a one-hand alphabet. The Abbé reasoned that the language of the hearing must be a foreign language to the deaf. Their first language then, gestural language, must therefore be used in their instruction.

The Abbé devised signs, which he called *signes méthodiques* (systematized signs), for certain functions of grammar. Writing, signing and finger-spelling were the major tools of his instruction.

De l'Epée held his classes for the deaf in a house he owned on the Rue des Moulins. More and more pupils came to the school until it became the world's first larger institute for under-privileged deaf children. Here they were educated, fed and clothed and the Abbé was like a father to them.

The Abbé put almost all of his fortune into the deaf school, keeping only a very modest amount, which he never allowed himself to exceed, for his personal needs. In the harsh winter of 1788, the Abbé refused to heat his apartments because of the high price of fuel and it was only after the tearful pleading of the forty students headed by the housekeeper that he consented to exceed his personal budget by three hundred livres. The aged and ailing de l' Épée could never forgive himself for this and was known to say, "I have stolen three hundred livres from my students."

In an effort to guarantee education for all deaf people, de l'Épée strove for the status of national institute for his school.

He never saw the realization of this dream, for not until two years after his death was the *Institut Nationale des Sourds-Muets* granted a government subsidy.

Abbé de l'Épée's teaching method formed a new school of thought in the field of deaf education. His method was called the French method and was based on writing, signing and finger-spelling.

Many school founders visited de l'Épée's school in Paris and adopted the French method for their own schools. Some of these were:

Mass and Augustin from Paris

Mouriez from le Mans

Ferrrand from Chartnes

Dubourg from Toulouse

Huby from Rouen

Sicard from Bordeaux

Salvau from Rome

Mademoiselle Blouin from Augers

Abbé Storck from Vienna

Sylvestre from Rouen, Italy

Ulrich from Geneva, Switzerland

Guyot from Groningen, Holland

D'Angulo and d'Aléa from Spain

Müller from Mainz, Germany

and Michel from Sardinia.

De l'Épée was a prolific writer and his keen perceptiveness is still admired today.

Abbé de l'Épée died on December 23, 1789 and was laid to rest in the Saint Nicolas Chapel at the church of Saint-Roche on February 1, 1790. In the year 1791 he was proclaimed "Benefactor of Mankind" by the French National Assembly.

Samuel Heinicke

Samuel Heinicke, 1729-90, Germany

Samuel Heinicke was born in 1729 in the Saxon town of Weissenfels. His father was a farmer. Samuel did not want to follow in his father's footsteps. Due to conflicts in the family he joined the army in Dresden. In his free time he studied mathematics, music, French and Latin. He wrote a great deal. Aside from his own studies, he tutored younger students. He resigned from the military around 1754. He started to tutor a deaf boy, first using writing and then speech by the Amman method.

This, however, was interrupted by the Seven-Year War (1756 to 1763). Heinicke, who had been reconscripted, was taken prisoner by the Prussians. He escaped and lived unobtrusively for some years.

After leaving the University of Jena, he became secretary to a Count Schimmelmann in Hamburg. In 1769, Heinicke became an organist and cantor in the village of Eppendorf near Hamburg. He taught at a public school and also took on deaf students whom he taught by the oral method.

He claimed that permitting the students to use sign language would inhibit their progress in speech. The sole tool of deaf education must therefore be the spoken word. By 1774 he had five deaf students in his school. One of them, a gifted girl,

The hand-written title page of Samuel Heinicke´s treatise, Arcanum from 1772.

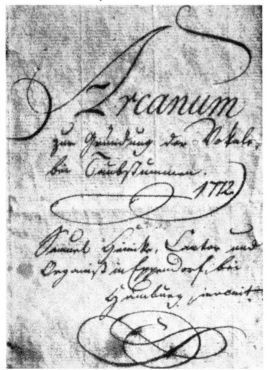

was the daughter of a Russian count.

After some time. Heinicke became interested in starting an institute for the deaf. Schimmelmann offered to find a building and seek public funding for this project in a provincial town, but Heinicke declined his offer. He wanted to establish his institute in a bigger city.

With the sponsorship of the Elector Friedrich August of Saxony, an institute for the deaf was founded in Leipzig in 1778. It was Germany´s first institute for the deaf. From the start it had nine students. The Elector visited the institute and then consented to sponsor the tuition of a number of underprivileged students, bringing the total number to fifteen.

Heinicke followed the Amman method, i.e. the oral method, modelling his own version of it as he went along. According to Heinicke, it is only by learning articulated speech that a deaf person gains a position in hearing society. Heinicke´s oralism precluded all sign language, gesticulation or finger-spelling. A new trend in deaf education, called the "German School", the German method or oral method, was born.

At first, Heinicke waited to teach his students speech until they had learned language through gestures and writing; but he soon revised his theories. Amman´s method had convinced him that the major emphasis must be on the spoken word. Heinicke used speech machines to demonstrate the proper position of the vocal organs for articulation.

In 1772, Heinicke wrote his treatise entitled *Arcanum* in which he associated the pronunciation of various vowel sounds with certain flavors. According to

Arcanum, deaf students could grasp the pronunciation of vowel sounds with the aid of their taste buds. They were given various liquids to taste and then told to say the vowel sounds:

i - sour vinegar
e - vermouth extract
ae - wormwood extract
a - pure water
o - sugar water
u - olive oil

Heinicke remained convinced of the value of *Arcanum* for the rest of his life. By the time of his death, in April of 1790, one hundred students had attended his institute.

The Letters of Abbé de l'Épée and Samuel Heinicke in Brief

In 1782, Abbé de l'Épée and Samuel Heinicke began a correspondence in which they argued for their respective methods of deaf education: the French method opposed to the German one. The two methods were presented to the Academy in Zurich for a verdict. Perhaps because Heinicke´s report on his method was incomplete, the Academy ruled in de l´Épée´s favor. One of the pamphlets in which the Abbé vehemently defended his method was *La Véritable Maniére d' Instruire les Sourds et Muets, Confirmée par une Longue Expérience*, written in 1776 and revised in 1784.

In his first letter to Samuel Heinicke, Abbé de l'Épée describes his visual method of teaching the deaf. Heinicke replied in German and the Abbé found it very difficult to read his letter. The rest of their correspondence was written in Latin. Abbé de l'Épée argued for the visual and Samuel Heinicke for the oral method. Heinicke wanted to demonstrate the oral method to Abbé de l'Épée and teach him to use it. He invited him to visit his institute warning him that it would take at least six months to truly learn the oral teaching method. De l'Épée declined this invitation, because to him the visual method was far superior. (See appendix for the letters)

Jean Marc Gaspard Itard, 1775-1838, France

The French physician, Jean Marc Gaspard Itard is considered one of the fathers of modern otolaryngology (the study of the ear, nose and throat) and was the first

Jean Marc Gaspard Itard

doctor to work with the school for the deaf in Paris.

In 1821 he published a major work, *Traité des Maladies de l'Oreille et de l'Audition* (Treatise on Diseases of the Ear and Hearing).

Itard defined five categories according to hearing disability:

1. Those who can hear human language, spoken slowly, clearly and at close range;
2. Those who can hear vowels but not consonants;
3. Those who can hear only some vowel sounds;
4. Those who can hear only loud noises (thunder, gunfire, etc.);
5. Those who are totally deaf.

Categories 1 to 3 represent 10%; category 4, 40% and category 5, 50% of all deaf people. This classification system has later been revised many times.

In 1880, the Germans divided the degree of residual hearing of the deaf into four classes:

1. Word hearing
2. Vowel hearing
3. Hearing a bell close to the ear
4. No hearing at all.

Itard´s teaching method

Itard taught only students belonging to the 10% of deaf people in his first three categories. Today we would call his students hearing impaired rather than deaf.

He was the first to use a special teaching method for certain groups of pupils depending on their hearing status. He started by training their hearing, but soon observed that the ability to discern sounds quickly did not necessarily mean the students started to speak.

When he introduced speech training, he noticed the students had trouble speaking spontaneously; they tried to sign with their hands all the time they were supposed to be speaking.

Itard regarded sign language as an obstacle to spontaneous speech. It was his opinion that the use of signed language by deaf students delayed their speech. Their speech was inferior. In order to improve it, Itard recommended that sign language among the students be forbidden.

Itard bequethed funds to the school of the deaf in Paris to set up an articulation class, where all instruction was to be given by his method. No signing was allowed there.

Auguste Bébian, 1789-1838, France

At the age of twelve, Auguste Bébian came to the school for the deaf in Paris, headed by his relative, Abbé Sicard who succeeded the late Abbé de l'Épée. Himself hearing, Young Bébian got to know the deaf students and learned sign language. He gradually mastered the teaching methods used at the school.

In the few years he practised as a teacher himself, he developed a method so radically different from those otherwise in

French Educational Charts from 1863

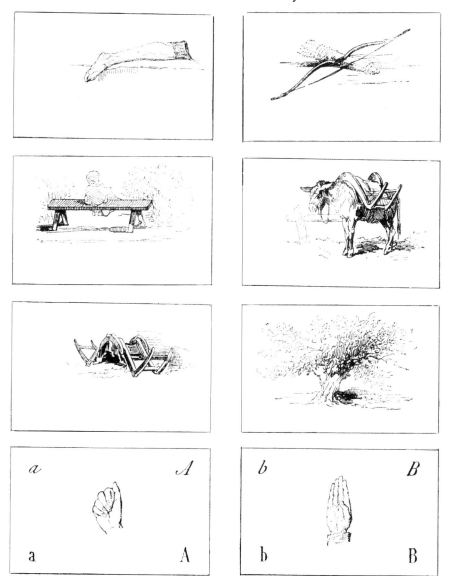

use that it brought him some enemies. He wanted to use deaf people´s own sign language in the classroom. Bébian´s contribution can be summarized in the following three points.

1. The rights of the deaf student must be respected by the staff of the boarding school. They must realize that they are there for the students instead of vice versa.

2. Bébian was the first to attempt to

describe sign language in linguistic terms. He introduced normative sign language grammar and invented a system for writing sign language.

3. Bébian´s aim was to offer all deaf people an education and the opportunity to develop their minds in all areas. This was to be done with the aid of the sign language of the deaf. The language they use to communicate with each other should also be used in the classroom.

In 1825, Bébian wrote *Mimographie*, the first attempt ever made to transcribe sign language.

Bébian believed deaf students should learn to write French before going on to spoken French, that is, speech and lipreading.

If the sign language of the deaf was to be used in the classroom, the teachers should be deaf themselves. More and more deaf people became teachers. In the mid-nineteenth century, approximately one third of all teachers of the deaf were deaf.

In summary, we can say that today´s debate in the field of deaf education to a large extent entails a revival of Bébian´s ideas. The sign language of the deaf was the basis for the theories of both Abbé de l'Épée and Bébian. Bébian´s aim was bilingualism.

Government Initiatives to Establish Schools for the Deaf in Europe

Schools for the deaf were started with the help of national governments.

1. Already existing schools were made state institutes, for example the Paris institute, nationalized in 1791 and the Berlin institute in 1798.

2. The national government aided in the establishment of schools for the deaf, for example in Stockholm in 1809.

3. The government provided deaf education programmes, for example in Schleswig-Holstein from 1805 and in the rest of Denmark from 1807. In Bavaria, legislation of 1817 required every province to have a deaf school, which lead to the establishment of five deaf schools during the following few years.

4. Publically financed schools for the deaf were started on the initiative of crowned heads of state, as in Vienna, St. Petersburg and Lisbon.

Abbé Sicard

The Decline of the French Method
Abbé Sicard, 1742 -1822, France

In the year 1786, Abbé Sicard, trained as a teacher of the deaf by Abbé de l'Épée, opened a school in Bordeaux. The French revolution broke out in 1789 and Abbé de l'Épée died the same year. In 1790, Sicard was appointed by the National Assembly to succeed him as director of the school for the deaf in Paris. In 1791, the Paris school moved to a new building and was granted the status of National Institute.

In the Terror of 1792, Sicard was arrested because he was a priest. He barely escaped the guillotine and went into hiding. However, some time later he was able to return to the Institute and resume teaching there.

According to Sicard, the deaf had no language and were therefore incapable of thinking. This view was characteristic of what was later termed oralism. Sicard wanted to give his students language and encourage them to think. Rejecting de l'Épée's exercises in writing from dictation, he emphasized more independent school work in the hopes of boosting the students' linguistic confidence. This method did not, however, prove entirely successful.

In 1794 Abbé Sicard transferred his teaching work to the Saint Magloire Seminary, now called the Saint Jaques Institute. Sicard was one of the foremost linguists of his time. He modified de l'Épée's sign language in an effort to improve upon it, but only succeeded in complicating it.

In 1808, Sicard published his great work, *Theorie des Signes*, a grammar and dictionary of sign language.

The Beginnings of European Schools for the Deaf

In its early history, education of the deaf in Europe was in the form of private tutoring. It was governed by no general regulations. The first schools for the deaf were established in the late eighteenth century. Of the schools listed below, the one founded by Abbé de l'Épée in Paris in 1770 is considered the first in the world. It was the first large deaf school with a set curriculum and open to all underprivileged deaf children.

59

Schools for the Deaf in Europe

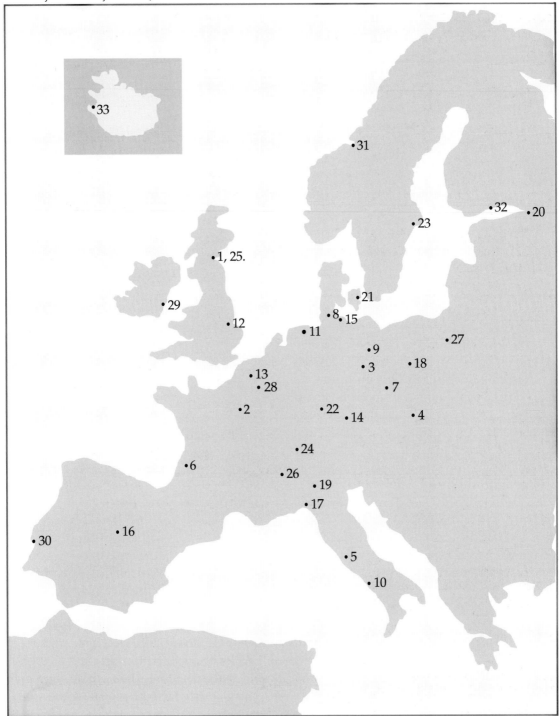

Some schools for the deaf established between 1760 and c. 1860

1. Scotland. Edinburgh 1760. Founder, Thomas Braidwood.
2. France. Paris 1770. Founder, Abbé de l' Épée.
3. Germany. Leipzig 1778. Founder, Samuel Heinicke.
4. Austria. Vienna 1779. Founder, Storck.
5. Italy. Rome 1784. Founder, Silvestri.
6. France. Bordeaux 1786. Founder, Sicard.
7. Czechoslovakia. Prague 1786. Founder, Berger.
8. Germany. Schleswig-Holstein 1787.
9. Germany. Berlin 1788. Founder, Eschke.
10. Italy. Naples 1789. Founder, Cozzolino.
11. Holland. Groeningen 1790. Founder, Guyot.
12. England. London 1792. Founder, John Townsend.
13. Belgium. Tournai 1793. (Closed soon after).
14. Germany. Munich 1798. Founder, Ernsdorfer.
15. Germany. Kiel 1799. Founder, Pfingsten.
16. Spain. Madrid 1800. Founder, Josep d'Aléa. Became a public school in 1814.
17. Italy. Genoa 1801. Founder, Assarotti.
18. Poland. Breslau (now Wroclaw) 1804. Founder, Bürgel.
19. Italy. Milan 1805. Founder, Eyrand.
20. Russia. St. Petersburg 1806. Founder, Siegmund.
21. Denmark. Copenhagen 1806. Founder, Castberg.
22. Germany. Gmünd, Württemberg 1807.
23. Sweden. Stockholm 1808. Founder, Pär Aron Borg.
24. Switzerland. Zurich 1809. Founder, Scherr.
25. Scotland. Edinburgh 1810. Founder, de Lys.
26. Switzerland. Moudon 1811.
27. Poland. Warsaw 1817. Founder, Falkowsky.
28. Belgium. Lüttich 1817.
29. Ireland. Dublin 1819.
30. Portugal. Lisbon 1824. Founder, Pär Aron Borg.
31. Norway. Trondheim 1824 Founder, Andreas Møller.
32. Finland. Borgå 1846. Founder, Malm.
33. Iceland. Reykjavik 1867. Founder, Séra Páll Pálsson.

Schools for the deaf were also founded outside Europe, for example in Hartford, Connecticut (U.S.A.) in 1817 by Gallaudet and Clerc and in Calcutta, India in 1828 by the Englishman, Nicolls.

The Decline of the German Method Dieter Eschke, 1766-1811, Germany

Heinicke´s son-in-law, Dieter Eschke, having trained as a teacher of the deaf in Vienna and Leipzig, founded an institute for the deaf in Berlin in 1788. After the death of Heinicke in 1790, the Berlin Institute became the deaf education center for all of northern Germany and a mother institute for the German method. Nationalized in 1798, it became the Royal Institute in Berlin and from 1812, Prussia´s major center for training teachers of the deaf.

After the death of Heinicke, Eschke took over the role of leading defender of the German method in Berlin and Leipzig. Sign language soon won a greater following

Eschke

in Germany. Deaf education was now under the influence of the French method, which was influencing deaf education in more and more countries.

Petschke, Germany

Heinicke´s successor at the school for the deaf in Leipzig, Petschke was in complete agreement with the method he had learned fully from him. Due to poor health, Petschke was not able to pass the method on to future generations. Thus, Heinicke´s method vanished.

The Next Generation of Schools

a) *Schools directly influenced by the French method through students of either de l'Épée or Sicard:*

1. The Viennese school, which from its seat in Vienna had a great influence throughout the Austro-Hungarian Empire
2. The Swiss school
3. The Dutch school with its headquarters in Groeningen
4. The Genoese school, from which deaf education spread to the rest of Italy
5. The American school with its methods imported from France

b) *Schools indirectly influenced by the French method, having adopted its principles:*

6. The Castberg School in Copenhagen, influencing in its turn the development of deaf education in Denmark,

Norway, and to some extent Sweden

7. The first Swedish school for the deaf in Stockholm, also influencing the development of deaf education in Finland, and Portugal

c) One Follower of the German method

was the Schlesian school where deaf education was introduced in the Duchies of Schleswig-Holstein.

Thomas Hopkins Gallaudet, 1787-1851, USA

The idea of a school for the deaf in the United States originated in the beginning of the nineteenth century.

Ever since 1679, various attempts had been made to train the deaf. Up until the nineteenth century, wealthy Americans had sent their deaf children to Europe for an education. A deaf nephew of President Monroe attended school in Paris. Many Americans attended the Braidwood Academy in Edinburgh or, after it was moved, in London.

In Hartford, Connecticut there lived a doctor by the name of Mason Cogswell whose daughter Alice had been deafened by scarlet fever at the age of two. Her speech soon deteriorated. Rather than send Alice to Europe, however, Cogswell wanted to start a school for the deaf in America. To find out how many deaf children were of school age, Cogswell asked pastors to count the deaf people in their parishes. In the year 1812, there were 84 deaf people in Connecticut and approximately two thousand in all of the United States.

In 1815, Cogswell called a meeting of ten of Hartford´s leading citizens to discuss the prospect of opening a school for the deaf. At this meeting it was decided that a collection should be made to send some appropriate person to Europe to study the education of the deaf. Two days later the young preacher, Thomas Hopkins Gallaudet was appointed for this task. He embarked for England a month later.

Born in Philadelphia, but a resident of Hartford since his youth, Gallaudet was an acquaintance of Cogswell´s. He had begun tutoring Alice from a book by Abbé Sicard. Although he had no intention of becoming a teacher of the deaf, Gallaudet

Thomas H. Gallaudet

Mason Cogswell

consented to make the trip to Europe.

Gallaudet planned to combine in the American school the best of both the French and the English teaching methods.

Once in England, he discovered that the Braidwood dynasty had monopolized deaf education and was not about to share its secrets. The only way for Gallaudet to learn this method would have been to work for three years at the Academy as an assistant teacher with an eleven-hour work day, an offer he declined. At the same time, Abbé Sicard, de l'Épée's successor at the Paris school, happened to be in London on a lecture tour. Sicard immediately invited Gallaudet to Paris for a crash course in the French method.

Three months later, Gallaudet returned to America, bringing with him a member of Sicard's faculty, Laurent Clerc, himself deaf. They arrived in the US in 1816, after a fifteen-month absence on the part of Gallaudet.

Clerc turned out to be invaluable as a living advertisement for what deaf education, in particular the French method, could do for the deaf. His first assignment was as the tutor of General Grant's niece, who became extremely proficient in the finger language.

Funded by private donations as well as by tax money, the first permanent school for the deaf, The American Asylum was opened in Hartford in the year 1817 with Alice Cogswell as one of its students. Thus the concept of a public school for the deaf and the French method were imported to the United States.

Gallaudet was director of the the school until 1830 when he resigned to become a hospital chaplain. His sons followed in their father's footsteps as educators of the deaf.

Laurent Clerc

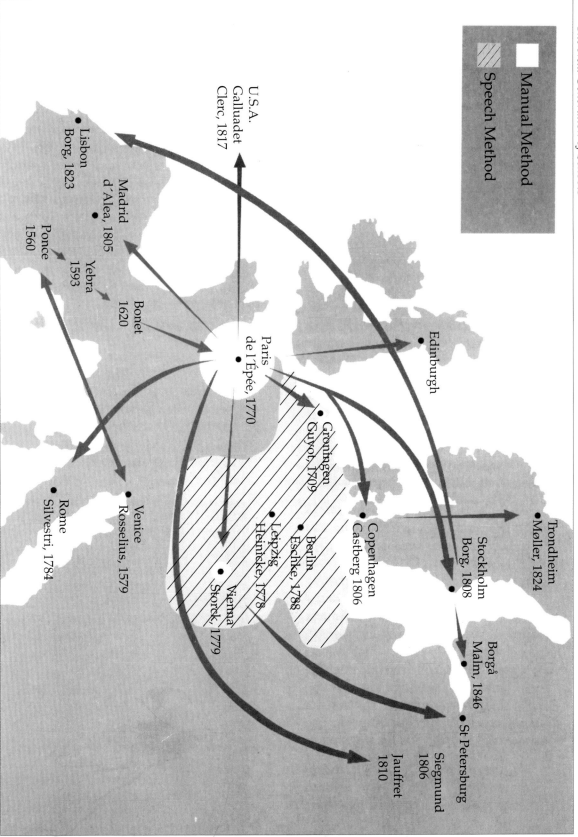

The Next Generation of Schools

Manual Method

Speech Method

U.S.A.
Galludet
Clerc, 1817

Lisbon
Borg, 1823

Madrid
d'Alea, 1805

Ponce
1560

Yebra
1593

Bonet
1620

Rome
Silvestri, 1784

Venice
Rosselius, 1579

Paris
de l'Épée, 1770

Edinburgh

Groningen
Guyot, 1709

Copenhagen
Castberg 1806

Berlin
Eschke, 1788

Leipzig
Heinicke, 1778

Vienna
Storck, 1779

Trondheim
Møller, 1824

Stockholm
Borg, 1808

Borgå
Malm, 1846

St Petersburg
Siegmund
1806

Jauffret
1810

German Educational Charts from the 1830s

German Educational Charts from the 1830s

The Dutch Hand Alphabet 1823

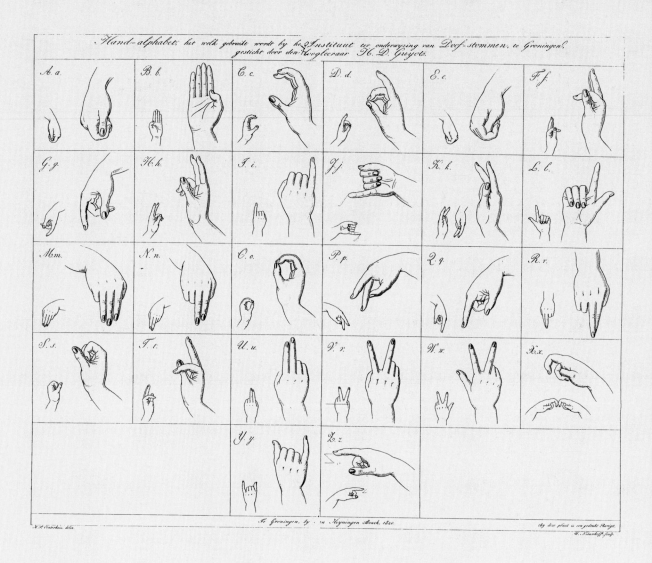

The Belgian Hand Alphabet 1844

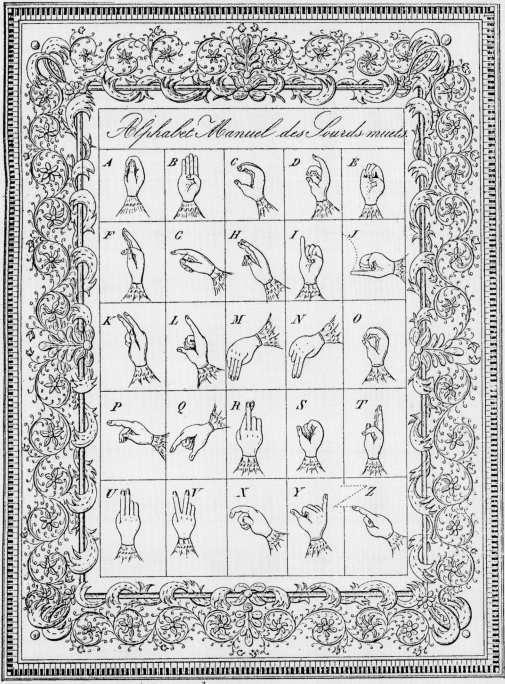

Alphabet Manuel des Sourds muets

Fait a l'Institut des Sourds-muets

The French Hand Alphabet 1834

Alphabet manuel

Imp: Lith: du Com rue St Nicolas Nancy

Finger-Spelled Words in French 1834

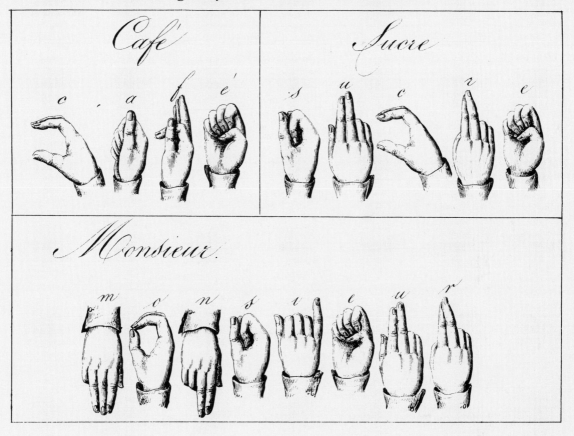

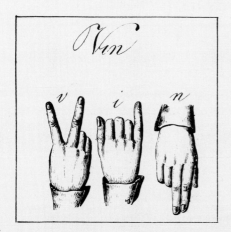

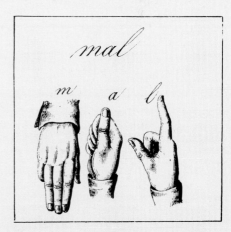

Numerals in the French Sign Language of 1863

Plates from F. H. Czech´s Book, Vienna, Austria 1836

The plates Franz Herrmann Czech included in his book, *Versinnlichte Denk- und Sprachlehre* (Visualized Mental and Oral Exercises) of 1836 were designed to help deaf students understand the grammar of written German. The figures on pages 73 through 81 show excerpts from this book. Tables 5 and 6 are aids for speech practice.

Plate from F. H. Czech´s Book

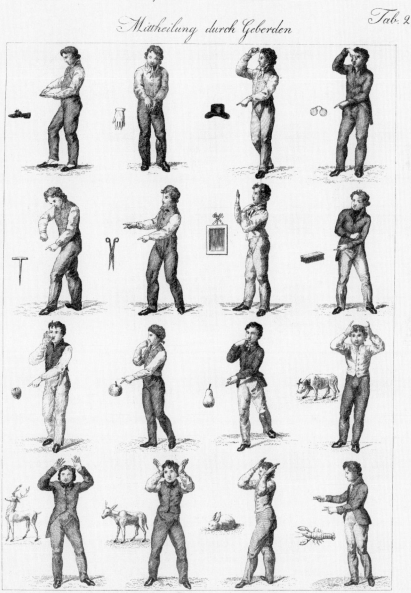

Plate from F. H. Czech´s Book

Tab. 3.

Schrift=und Handzeichen für articulirte Laute

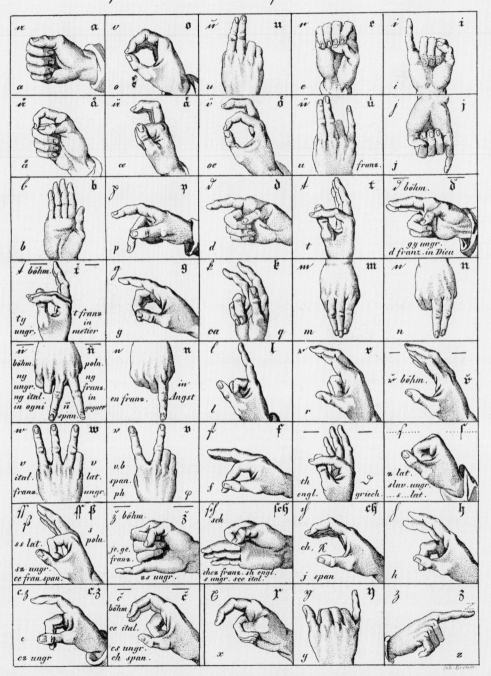

Plate from F. H. Czech´s Book

Mundlagen bei der Aussprache der Buchstaben
a, o, u, w, v, f, c, i, b, p.

Tab. 5.

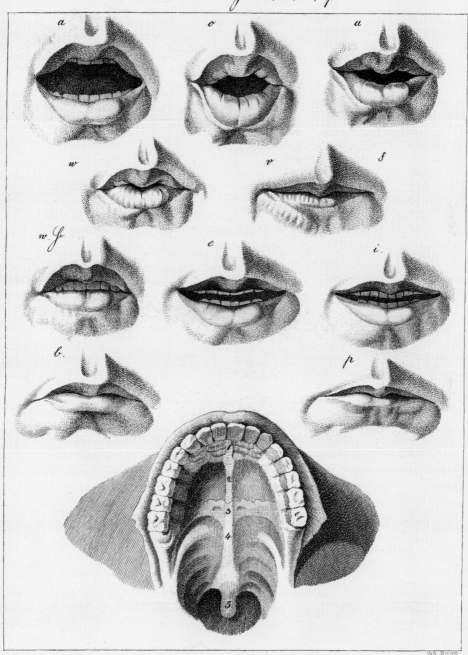

Plate from F. H. Czech´s Book

Mundlagen bei der Aussprache der Buchstaben. Tab. 6.
m , n. l. d. t. g . k. s . sch . ch . r .

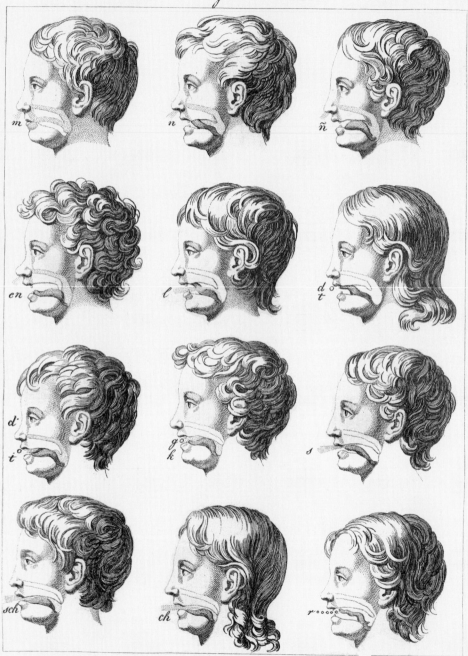

Plate from F. H. Czech´s Book

Tab. 8

Fragewörter.

Plate from F. H. Czech´s Book

Begriff und Bezeichnung der Vorwörter: auf, unter, über, an, in, bei, aus, vor, hinter, nach, neben, gegen, zu.

Tab. 32.

Plate from F. H. Czech´s Book

Plate from F. H. Czech´s Book

Drawings from F. H. Czech´s Book

Some European Schools Founded on the French Method

The Genoese School

Ottavio Assarotti founded Italy´s third school for the deaf in Genoa in 1804. The schools for the deaf in Rome (founded in 1784) and Naples (founded in 1788) did not prove as important to the future of Italian deaf education as the school in Genoa. Assarotti was impressed by the French method which he knew from his correspondence with Sicard. However, Assarotti was also of the opinion that "the best method is no method at all"; the best school being the school of life.

Major successors to Assarotti were Boselli, Fabriani and Pendola.

Boselli became famous for a book in which he condemned the oral method in no uncertain terms.

Fabriani conducted in depth studies of the logic of grammar while developing a pantomimic style of teaching.

Pendola, working as a teacher in Siena, introduced the oral or speech method there in 1872.

The Castberg School

Castberg's system, used in Denmark and Norway, stressed spiritual guidance and language learning. Classes were conducted in sign language. Castberg was also an important influence on Swedish deaf education between the years 1817 and -19.

The First School for the Deaf in Sweden

In 1808, Pär Aron Borg founded a private school for the deaf in Stockholm. In 1809-10, it became a national institute. Here there was a stronger emphasis on practical skills than on book-learning. Gestural language was used.

A Summary of Four Different Teaching Systems

Between 1760 and 1880 various methods of deaf education were in use: the sign language method, the speech method or the writing method. There were four systems.

1. The writing system (the Spanish system).
   Thomas Braidwood refined the system Wallis had originally adopted from Bonet and Ponce de León.
   Using a hand alphabet, the students were taught to:
   A. Write and then pronounce single letters,
   B. Write and then pronounce whole words.

2. The manual system (the French system).
   Starting with Bonet´s hand alphabet, Charles-Michel de l'Épée developed a language of signs. Spoken language was a foreign language to the deaf. All teaching was to be done in sign language.

3. The oral system (the German system).
   Amman´s successor, Samuel Heinicke,

82

became the advocate of the oral system in Germany. Articulated speech was the only means of communication permitted. Signs, gestures or finger-spelling had no place in the classroom.

4. The combined system (Deschamps´ system).
   Claude Francois Deschamps´ method was to combine the above mentioned systems. He used systematized signs, writing, lipreading and finger-spelling.

Until the Second Congress of Teachers of the Deaf in Milan in 1880, the sign language (French) system and the oral (German) system were predominant.

Why did Speech Training (the German system) Prevail at the Second Congress Teachers of the Deaf in Milan in 1880?

The French revolution broke out on July 14, 1789 and in 1804 Napoleon Boneparte took power. French armies marched across Europe. All that was modern in France at the time, including the French deaf education method, spread to other countries. However, when Napoleon was defeated in 1814, everything French was regarded with distaste.

In 1814-15, the Vienna Convention drew up new borders in Europe. The German Federation was created, consisting of thirty-eight states instead of the previous number of over four hundred. Nationalism began to grow in Germany during the Napoleonic wars leading to greater unity. The Germans had a strong sense of order. In the year 1871, the Federation of German Republics consisted of twenty-five states ruled by Otto von Bismarck, the "Iron Chancellor".

The first teacher of the deaf to revive the German teaching method was the German, Johann Baptist Graeser (1766-1841). Like Samuel Heinicke, he thought the only way for a deaf person truly to become a member of society was by learning to converse as though he were hearing. Gestural language had to be avoided entirely.

Also at this time, the French started to abandon gestural language. The German system was becoming more and more prevalent in the deaf schools of France. Speech was already being taught at the Paris school in de l'Épée´s time and in 1839 speech training was introduced in Bordeaux.

Teachers at that time knew that deaf students might receive an inferior education by the oral method. Why, then, was it used? Since deafness was medically incurable, it was believed that deaf people should be made to speak in order to be normal.

At that time, the degree of a hearing disability could not be measured. Anyone whose hearing was at all abnormal was called deaf. No deaf community was allowed to exist. The non-hearing were regarded as potentially hearing and should therefore speak. All deaf children had to be trained to speak. Sign language was not considered a viable means of conveying information.

Advocates of the oral method claimed:
a) that "the pure oral method" was

essential to the physical well-being of the deaf,

b) that sign lanuguage could not be used as a teaching language, and

c) that speech was a gift of God.

Tuberculosis (TB) was more common among deaf than hearing children. This was believed to be because deaf children used their lungs wrongly, but the real reason was the unsanitary living conditions at boarding schools. It was not until the end of the nineteenth century that the cause of tuberculosis and how it was transmitted came to be known.

Victor August Jäger, a German teacher of the deaf, published an attack on sign language and finger-spelling. He was also opposed to the segregation of the deaf. Another teacher of the deaf, Friedrich Moritz Hill (1805-74), also German and an advocate of the oral method, had a great deal of influence on deaf education. He was an educator of teachers for the deaf.

One of Hill´s followers was David Hirsch (1813-96), director of the school for the deaf in Rotterdam for thirty-five years. In 1861, the Italian priest Abbé Balestre (1834-86) visited Hirsch and then spread the oral method in his own country. The most important person he persuaded to convert to the oral method was Abbé Giulo Tarra (1832-89), the director of the school for the deaf in Milan. The German method was so prevalent around this time because Germany now dominated Europe as a result of her victory over France in the war of 1870-71.

The First Congress of Teachers of the Deaf was held in Paris in 1878. Even ten years after the Franco-German war, it was impossible to speak of a German teaching method in France. The very name of the method turned people against it.

At the Second Congress for Teachers of the Deaf in Milan in 1880, the method was no longer referred to as the German method, but rather as the "pure oral method". 255 delegates from countries with deaf schools all over the world attended the congress. 157 of them were from Italy (98 from Milan), 67 from France, 12 from England, 8 from Germany, 6 from the United States and one each from Belgium, Canada, Norway, Russia and Sweden. The Swedish delegate was Carl Kierkegaard-Ekbohrn, principal of the Bollnäs School for Deaf Adults.

Program for Discussion at the Congress in Milan, 1880:

The Organization and Housing of Institutions for the Deaf and Dumb and the Materials Used

1. Should the institution have the form of a day school or boarding school? Discuss the advantages and inconveniences of each.

2. For a day school, there is only the matter of furnishing classrooms fulfilling sufficient sanitary standards to improve and preserve the students´ health, providing school materials, correctly placing blackboards, desks and benches etc.

3. For a boarding school, besides classrooms, the following must be provided:

   a. dormitories spacious enough to

accomodate a large number of children under acceptable sanitary conditions,

b. a dining hall,
c. a covered playground,
d. an infirmary,
e. one or two workshops suitably equipped for the deaf-mute to learn a trade within the school curriculum or through apprenticeship to individual craftsmen after leaving school,
f. lastly, large courtyards with equipment for gymnastics must be adjacent to a boarding school.

Instruction

1. How large ought the number of students at an institute for the deaf and dumb be? How many school masters and mistresses are required? What is the appropriate ratio of faculty to students?

2. At what age is it desirable for the deaf-mute to start school, whether the method used in the school be oral or through signs?

3. What physical and intellectual endowments does the deaf-mute need if he is to benefit from his education and acquire intelligible speech?

4. How many years of schooling are required for a deaf-mute to be educated by the oral method and by the sign-language method respectively?

5. Is it necessary to place congenitally deaf students in separate classes from those deafened by illness?

6. How many pupils can be effectively instructed at one time by a teacher using the oral method and how many by one using the sign-language method?

7. Is it more appropriate for the deaf-mute to have one and the same teacher throughout school, or to change teachers upon attaining a certain level of proficiency?

8. Should the students stand or sit during classes? Should they write on the blackboard as a rule, or on slates?

9. How long should each lesson be? Should there be a break between two lessons?

Methods

1. Describe the ways in which the oral method is preferable to the the sign-language method and vice versa (this applies particularly to the classroom situation, but also to the demands of every-day social intercourse).

2. Explain what is meant by the pure oral method and how it differs from the so called combined method.

3. What distinguishes conventional signs from natural ones?

4. What are the most natural and effective means by which the deaf-mute can

rapidly gain proficiency in normal language?

5. When and how should the deaf-mute be taught the grammar of the language, regardless of whether the oral or sign-language method is used?

6. At what point should the students be given textbooks?

7. Should not elementary drawing, i.e. the free-hand imagery of the forms of objects, constitute an integral part of the upbringing of a deaf-mute?

8. What can be learned by the deaf-mute in a given amount of time, if he is intructed by:
   a. the oral method,
   b. the sign-language method?

9. How should good discipline be attained at a school for the deaf and dumb?

Special Questions

1. Do the deaf and dumb, after leaving the institute, forget most of what they have learned if they have been taught by the oral method and do they resort to gestures and writing when conversing with people in possession of all their senses? If this is the case, why is this and how can the situation be remedied?

2. Where and how can young men who, due to their deafness, have been excluded from the pursuit of studies in the classics, be offered an education comparable to that offered in institutions of higher learning for youths with all their senses intact? Ought such an education be offered in a more advanced section of the school for the deaf and dumb or at a separate institution? Should the teachers on this level be teachers of the deaf and dumb or teachers of the fully endowed.

3. For what trades are deaf-mutes best suited; in what trades are they most successful and can new vocational paths be opened to them?

4. Are not the deaf and dumb more susceptible than the non-deaf to certain syndromes and diseases? Furthermore, considering the temperament of the deaf and dumb in general, should not special laws of hygiene be observed in their case and special forms of therapy be used?

5. Does the latest census in any European country show an increase or decrease in the ratio of the deaf and dumb to the entire population of the country in question? If either of these tendencies can be observed, what are the reasons for it?

The Milan congress was chaired by Abbé Tarra who had converted to the oral method of teaching some years earlier. He lead heated discussions on the pros and cons of the oral method. Reports from advocates of the one method or the other were read from the podium. Some suggested a combination of oral and manual methods. The oral method prevailed. The following resolution was adopted through an overwhelming majority:

The Congress, considering the incontestable superiority of speech over signs in restoring the deaf mute to society, and in giving him a more perfect knowledge of language, declares that the oral method ought to be preferred to that of signs for the education and instruction of the deaf and dumb. Source : Wright, D. Deafness. a Personal Account, London 1969. p.177.

Conclusions from the Congress
(as recorded by Kierkegaard-Ekbohrn):

1. The spoken word being indisputably superior to sign language in reinstating the deaf-mute in society while providing him with proficiency in language, the suitable method of education and cultivation of the deaf and dumb is the oral rather than the pantomimic method.

2. Considering the detrimental effect the simultaneous use of speech and signs has on speech, lipreading ability and lucidity of thought, the pure method (free from sign language) is to be preferred in the instruction of the deaf and dumb.

3. Although one purpose of the pure oral teaching method is to give deaf and dumb students an education as much as possible like that of the fully endowed, the Congress deems the most natural and effective technique in the education of the deaf and dumb to be illustration, i.e. depicting, first with the spoken word and then in writing, the objects placed or actions carried out before the eyes of the deaf students.

4. As it has been repeatedly shown that deaf-mutes of varying social standing who have graduated from the institutes have, upon being questioned on a wide variety of topics, replied correctly and with a clear enough pronunciation after easily reading the lips of the questioner, the Congress concludes that the deaf-mute educated by the pure oral method does not forget what he has learned at the institute, but rather further enhances his skills through conversation and reading. Furthermore, it has been found that these deaf-mutes use speech exclusively and, thus, far from losing this ability, constantly improve it along with the skill of lipreading through everyday use.

5. An education of the deaf and dumb by the oral method should be begun between the ages of eight and ten years.

6. The deaf and dumb should attend school for at least seven or eight years.

7. A teacher using the pure oral method can have no more than ten pupils at one time.

The Third Period of Deaf Education, after 1880

In the first phase of the history of deaf education, before 1760, deaf students were tutored privately. In the second period, between 1760 and 1880, shools for the deaf were established. There was a debate about which of the two methods, oral or manual, was the best. At the Milan Congress in 1880, the oral method won the day. In the third period, from 1880 onwards, three main methods have been in use: the oral method, the writing method and the sign-language method. The oral method has become predominant.

Different Philosophies in the Third Period of Deaf Education

1. Speech should be used in the instruction of all deaf students.

2. All the more educable students should be taught using speech, the others with gestures.

3. All educable deaf students should be instructed using writing.

4. The most educable deaf students should be instructed using speech, and the least educable with gestures.

Characteristic of the beginning of the third period is that national governments took charge of and legally regulated deaf education. Each country having its own legal system, different types of school and school systems developed. In Europe education became accessible to all deaf children. Deaf education became mandatory.

Denmark

Denmark was the leading country in this area. Already in the second period in the history of deaf education, in 1805, a mandatory school for the deaf was started in Schleswig-Holstein and in 1817 deaf education became mandatory in the rest of Denmark. (Until conquered by Prussia in 1864, Schleswig-Holstein was Danish.)

Germany

The first German states to start schools for the deaf were: Saxony in 1873, Saxony-Weimar-Eisenach 1874, Oldenburg 1876, Saxony-Koburg-Gotha in 1877, Anhalt in 1884, Braunschwieg in 1894 and Prussia in 1912.

Norway

In Norway, deaf education became mandatory with the 1883 law "pertaining to schools for abnormal children".

Britain

In England and Scotland school for the deaf became mandatory in the 1890s.

France

In 1906, the French government ruled on the establishment of public schools for the deaf and blind in accordance with a law of 1882. French schools for the deaf thereby ceased to be charitable institutions. By the year 1914, there were National Institutes for the Deaf in Paris, Bordeaux and Savoyen. The Institute in Paris was for boys and the one in Bordeaux for girls. Besides these, there were four or five other schools for the deaf in France. In all there were school places for 1,200 deaf children. In 1914 there were 5,000 deaf children of school age in France, which probably meant that many of them had to go without an education.

At the beginning of 1991, a new law was passed in France allowing parents to choose whether their children should be taught by the traditional oralist method or by a teacher fluent in sign language.

Finland

Education for the deaf in Finland became mandatory in 1918.

Sweden

On May 13th, 1889, deaf education became mandatory in Sweden. As early as 1862, Principal Ossian Edmund Borg had in-

Jehubba Blomkvist

Ola Kyhlberg

troduced the oral method at the Manilla School for the Deaf in Stockholm where previuosly the manual method had been used. Advocates of the oral method in the 1870s were Jehubba Blomkvist, principal of the school for the deaf in Örebro and Ola Kyhlberg, pricipal of Manilla School.

Jehubba Blomkvist had studied the German method in Germany. He believed that every educable deaf person should learn the language through the spoken word for the purpose of social contact with the hearing. Articulation was greatly emphasized in the classroom. Blomkvist claimed to achieve good results. He regarded finger language as the worst enemy of language and speech. Sign language was prohibited and students who used it were punished. He thought it was better for students to live away from the school, because that would bring them into contact with the hearing and force them to use their speech skills.

Ola Kyhlberg´s philosophy was that the oral method should be tried on all deaf students, but those who failed to learn to speak and lipread should be instructed using the written method, i.e. a combination of writing and finger-spelling. He thought that as much school work could be covered using the written method as by the oral method. The sign-language method should be used to teach mentally retarded deaf children. Kyhlberg´s method became the most widely used in Sweden. Students who could not learn to speak well enough were transferred to so called writing and signing classes, where the teacher wrote on the board and finger-spelled. Trainable mentally retarded deaf children were sent to a special school.

From 1938, exceptionally gifted students with good residual hearing were sent to the "Special School for the Not Genuinely Deaf and Dumb" in Örebro. After a month in the first grade of the ordinary deaf school, these children were specially selected and transferred to Örebro where only the pure oral method was used.

Sign language was marginalized when the students were divided up according to aptitude and it was only allowed in classes for the mentally retarded.

With the introduction of a new school form, the primary and lower secondary school for the deaf, in 1965, The Special School for the Not Genuinely Deaf and Dumb in Örebro became a regular school for the deaf. The oral method retained its stronghold in all Swedish schools for the deaf. The Swedish National Association of the Deaf fought for sign language in the deaf schools.

On the 14th of May 1981, a bill was passed in Sweden´s House of Parliament acknowledging the right of the deaf to bilingualism. Sign language was acknowledged as an official language and the first language of the deaf, Swedish as their second language.

The World

In most European countries and the United States, the deaf receive an education, usually by the oral method. Many schools are now using a variety of teaching methods and classroom languages. The level of education of deaf people varies greatly from one country to another, ranging from elementary school to university. However, in many countries of the world the deaf are offered no education. According to statistics presented at the World Congress of the Deaf in Japan in 1991, 80% of the deaf people in developing countries remain illiterate. It is difficult for these deaf people to control their own lives and earn a living.

The World´s First Professorship in Sign Language

The first sign language research project in Sweden was undertaken at the Department of Linguistics at the University of Stockholm commissioned by the Swedish National Board of Education.

On June 10, 1990, Sweden´s Parliament

Brita Bergman

authorized the establishment of a professorship in sign language. Sweden was the first country in the world to acknowledge the status of sign language in this way.

The president of the Swedish National Association of the Deaf, Anders Andersson, had this to say about the decision of Parliament:

" After many years of struggle for the acceptence of sign language, the ruling of the Parliamentary Commission on Education marks a victory for our Association. I view this legislation as a definite advocation and acknowledgement of sign language. This step forward made in Sweden is also a step forward for deaf people in other countries. The battle field of the enemies of sign language, the oralists, is shrinking considerably."

The first professorship in sign language in the world was created on July 1, 1990.

Dr. Brita Bergman, Ph.D. became the world´s first professor of sign language.

The Letters of Abbé de l'Épée and Samuel Heinicke

Abbé de l'Épée's first letter to Samuel Heinicke:

My dear Learned Gentleman,

Had you read my opus, published under the title of *Instruction of the Deaf and Dumb by Systematized Signs*, your letter to the Viennese teacher of the deaf and dumb would not have contained as many objections to the method employed by him; a method which is also mine. The signs we use for purposes of instruction are not, as you assume, hieroglyphs. On the contrary, we carefully select signs with a natural, or if I may say so, sensible relation to the objects they describe.

This claim is supported by the testimony of a highly learned and perceptive critic, the Abbé de Condillac, whose judgement is of the greatest weight in matters of science. Formerly the tutor of the Prince of Parma, he says, on page 11 of volume 1, part 1, chapter one of the fourteen-volume curriculum he compiled for the instruction of said young prince, in reference to our method of instruction for the deaf and dumb:

"The Parisian teacher of the deaf and dumb [de l'Épée] has transformed the language of signs into a systematized art, plain and simple, through which he relates to his pupils a wide variety of concepts; indeed, I do not hesitate to say, concepts more clear and concise than those acquired with the help of hearing. Since at an early age, we have no grasp of the meaning of words unless we consider the circumstances in which they are used, it often happens that, throughout our lives, we remain uncertain as to the original and genuine nuance of a particular word's meaning.

"Such is not the case with those deaf and dumb students who have been instructed through systematized signs. Their instructor has at his disposal a unique way to provide the pupils with an understanding of abstract concepts, namely the analysis that it is essential for him to carry out in the presence of the students, an art they gradually master themselves so that they can easily repeat the process of proceeding from the concrete to the abstract. From this one can deem the advantages of this kind of "talking" over the conventional spoken language used by our governesses and school masters."

Had you been acquainted with our method, you would not have questioned the Viennese teacher as to whether the deaf-mute, upon being presented with the sentence, *Apportez ce livre* and further, *Je voudrois que vous apportassiez ce livre*, would not be confused by the change in verb forms.

Not in the least, learned Sir! Our deaf-mute (if you will allow me to speak the language of grammar to a fellow grammarian) pointing with his little stick from one to the other of these lines so arranged on the board, would tell us that *apportez* is the present imperative form of the French verb, *apporter* [to bring], while *apportassiez* is the plural second person past subjunctive form of this transitive verb of the first conjugation. Further, the student will be able to inform us that the second person is used here because someone is being addressed; that the reason it is in the plural is that this is the polite form of address in our language (as is the third person plural in German); in the past tense because, due to the form of the preceeding expression of wish, the desired action, although in reality a thing of the future, is expressed in the past tense, the request having already been stated; the subjunctive form is used because the speaker is indirectly quoting himself making the tense of one verb dependent on that of another; finally, that we recognize this verb as belonging to the first conjugation by the fact that its infinitive form ends in -er *(apporter)*. All this will be told us by the deaf-mute in signs without the aid of the teacher. This will doubtlessly lead you to conclude that the student must be well-versed in the rules of conjugation.

If you had read our *Instruction* and, although it is written in French, understood it, your letter to the Viennese teacher of the deaf and dumb would not have contained the following three untrue statements: 1. Hearing cannot be replaced by vision.

2. Abstract concepts cannot, even with the help of writing and systematized signs, be made accessible to the mind of the deaf and dumb. 3. The students must forget very quickly the signs and the words he has learned through them.

From our book you would have learned that common words, singly as well as in context, are so indelibly imprinted on the minds of our pupils that they can immediately write them down from books or letters as they are dictated in systematized signs. His Majesty the Emperor, certainly an impartial observer, can verify this. [On May 7, 1777, the Emperor Franz Joseph II of Germany, disguised as Count von Falkenstein, visited de l'Épée's institute for the deaf and dumb on Rue des Moulins in Paris.] He noticed some sentences, written on our board in four languages. He merely glanced at them apparently assuming they had been written with the help of a teacher. Having gathered this from the expression on the face of the Emperor, I had the board wiped clean. Humbly addressing his Majesty, I asked that he be so kind as to hand me any epistle he might have on his person, so that I may dictate it in systematized signs and have the deaf-mutes accurately reproduce its contents in writing. He complied with my request and found no words to express his admiration for the results. I then asked if it would please his majesty to see one of the deaf-mutes recount the contents of said letter to one of his classmates in the same way. When this had been demonstrated, the Emperor was astounded. Do you believe, learned Sir, that any sensible teacher would embark on the type of excercise I conduct every day, if his pupils did not recall all the more commonly used words and were not sure of the rules of grammar which they have learned through systematized signs?

I should like to refer to another man´s testimony, a man of European acclaim, that is, M. Linguet who believed the deaf and dumb could never become anything but semi-automatons. Knowing he was of this opinion I wrote to him, among other things, the following:

"I cannot tolerate that you, such a renowned scientist, hold the way in which you yourself have attained the basis for your understanding of the world to be the only one possible and refuse to accept the existence of other, equally feasible ways. Does not reason itself tell us that there is no more intimate connection between concepts and the sounds that meet our ears than between concepts and the written signs we perceive with our eyes?" I proceeded to elaborate on this idea.

Hardly a fortnight later, M. Linguet paid me a visit. Interrupting my work, I asked him to name to me whatever abstract concepts he pleased, so that I could explain them to the deaf-mutes in systematized signs. As he insisted on giving me, although I tried to demur, the honor of making his choice, I suggested: *intellectus, intellectualis, intelligentia, intelligibilis, intelligibiliter, inintelligibiliter, inintelligibilitas* . These seven words, all pertaining to the function of the intellect, are expressed with different systematized signs. "Here, Sir, are abstract concepts from which you are welcome to choose freely". After some courteous remarks, he selected the word *inintelligibilitas*, assuming it to be the most difficult. Nonetheless, one of the deaf-mutes immediately wrote the correct word. While he examined this result with interest, I returned to the point of our contention. "It is not enough, good Sir, for you to see the word you chose was written by the student. I would also like to explain to you briefly how it is conveyed to the student in systematized signs. Five signs, the rapid execution of which you have seen, are sufficient to depict the word with the greatest accuracy.

"The first sign indicates that this is an inner, rather than an outer process. The second implies the mind´s ability to read to itself, i.e. its ability to understand what is presented to it. The third sign shows this ability as possible which gives us the adjective *intelligibilis*, which is then transformed by forth sign into the abstract noun *intelligibilitas*. Lastly, the fifth sign, a negation, renders *inintelligibilitas*."

After five or six more such experiments, this erudite witness of my credibility did not persist. When I invited him to do so, he said it would not be necessary, as he was now convinced that I could give account for each sign. There remained, however, one point he wished to investigate. That is, whether the deaf-mutes, having demonstrated such acute comprehension of the concepts expressed to them in systematized signs, could define the term "metaphysical".

In compliance with his request, I wrote on the board the question, "How would you describe a metaphysical concept?" While I went on talking to my visitor, paying no attention to how the students were coming along with the assignment, one of the deaf-mutes produced the following answer: "To me, metaphysical concepts are those concerning things independent of our senses, above our senses, which we cannot grasp with our senses, which do not in any way affect our senses."

Upon reading this reply, M. Linguet asked me to beg the

pardon of the deaf-mutes, whom he had doubtlessly offended by having referred to them as semi-automotons.

I then dictated, in systematized signs, the following sentences to the students : "This learned gentleman openly admits that he had actually been of the opinion which he expressed in writing about you. However, he now wishes to retract this remark."

In parting, he assured me he would puplicize what he had seen and heard. As everyone who reads newspapers knows, he cannot be held responsible for not having kept this promise. [Linguet was imprisoned shortly after his visit to de l'Épée.]

Were you familiar with our method, you would certainly have known that we always dictate moving our lips, but uttering no sound. Observers of our lessons can then hear nothing, but no single word eludes the deaf-mutes who grasp with their eyes what has escaped the hearing observers.

Although you have indeed, erudite Sir, opposed our method without being familiar with it, I honestly do not take offense. Quite on the contrary, I am delighted that there is at the Academy in Leipzig a learned gentleman dedicated to the same work as that to which I have entirely devoted so many years of my life. I close my letter and ask you please to pardon my verbosity. Should you be willing to subject yourself to the tedium of reading about my method and if you will promise to assist me with your advice, I would send to you a copy of my book. Oh! If someone were to find a surer and more convenient way, I would readily follow in his footsteps, gratefully acknowledging the favor.

May God preserve your health, learned Sir.

Your devoted servant,

*** Teacher of the deaf and dumb in Paris

The Parisian Teacher´s Second Letter to the Teacher of the Deaf and Dumb in Leipzig

I was unable to read your letter to me, written as it was in German and in a tiny hand. Had I read it, the task of translating it into French would have been strenuous and not altogether worthwhile. I had hoped, however, to find among those of your compatriots who often visit my lessons, one willing to read the German and relate to me in French the contents of your epistle .

   Some did attempt to tell me its contents, not in writing, but orally. They all gave up the task, however; no one has completed it. These hasty translations were hardly reliable and, due to the discrepancy between the printed and hand-written forms of your characters, my dictionaries were of no help in ascertaining whether or not the meaning of your words had been correctly interpreted.

   It is then through no fault of my own that I have delayed in responding to your criticism. I did immediately take pen in hand when a learned gentlemen who had not come to my attention, one greatly interested in the deaf and dumb and those who instruct them, did me the long awaited favor [of translating your letter].

   Since I am not fluent in German and you do not have a full command of French, we must resort to a language of which we both have a better and more complete knowledge. Hence I deemed it necessary to translate also my first letter to you from the original French into Latin. I am certain that you have understood neither my letter nor my book, for your letter contained many things you would not have written had you understood my French.

   There are three major matters about which we disagree, erudite Sir.

1. You believe that my method is identical with that publicized by the learned gentlemen, Wallis, Amman, and Bonet.

2. You assure us that you have discovered a shorter and more convenient approach to the education of the deaf and dumb. On this point you share the views of Péreire, until fairly recently an instructor of the deaf and dumb here.

3. You regard as impossible that which we demonstrate to learned men of all walks of life and from all countries every day in our public lessons.

I will only very briefly touch upon the first of these points. To me it is a matter of no importance whether I am regarded as the inventor of my method or thought to have drawn upon the work of others.

Nonetheless, to elucidate the matter, there has, to my knowledge, been no mention made of systematized signs, not even of the term itself, before me. No one has previously used such signs to represent visually not only the persons, but also the numbers, tenses, modes of verbs.

Furthermore, I know of no author who has devised a system by which a given characteristic sign can be inflected, not only indicating person, number, tense and mode in the case of verbs for which my system is a spring of possibilties, but also for nouns and in particular for adjectives and adverbs by adding grammatical signs to the root.

I have also found no one else able to demonstrate how, by analysis and the combination of different signs, even the metaphysical concepts used by philosophers can be presented so clearly to the eye that nothing is missed.

It would not offend me were someone today to mention systematized signs in his method of teaching the deaf and dumb and himself take credit for their invention. I do not seek personal fame, but rather strive for the well-being of humanity.

I am the inventor of this method; may anyone who wishes be given the credit for it.

Enough, now, about my method.

Secondly, you believe you have found a short and easy way of instructing the deaf and dumb. Your opinion is, then, that the students must be instructed in speech from the start, because that would give them more ready access to cultivation, than does my method, based on the written word and systematized signs.

You share, then, the views of Péreire, who in a book he wrote in French thirty years ago and presented to the Royal Academy of Sciences in Paris in the year 1751, refers to himself in the third person as follows:

"Péreire devides his instruction into two main parts, utterance and comprehension. In the first area, he imparts to his pupils the art of speaking and reading our mother tongue. He then explains to the deaf-mutes some of the most common expressions along with the names of every-day objects such as foods, pieces of clothing, and furniture.

In the second part, he teaches all the other language skills necessary to complete their schooling, that is, the meanings and peculiarities of words, so that the students themselves, with their knowledge of grammar and their own sense of the language can express themselves appropriately, be it orally or in writing.

After only a few days of practice, his pupils are capable of pronouncing some words clearly.

The first part of his instruction takes twelve or, at most, fifteen months, particularly if the students are of a tender age. The second part, however, requires more time to be done thoroughly."

Thus the method of Péreire. He will forgive me for saying that it is exceedingly detrimental to the progress of the students in that it lets their minds go without nourishment for twelve to fifteen months.

Our instruction of the deaf and dumb takes an entirely different course, following the example set by our own child-hood teachers. These individuals may have been those actually charged with our up-bringing or else servants, older brothers or relatives, who not consciously, but nonetheless in some way, imparted knowledge to us at every moment throughout our childhood.

It would have been to no avail for these family mentors merely to identify and name the objects around us without causing us to cast an eye on them through a movement of the hand or some other visible clue.

This vulgar method of instruction, as it were, borrowed from nature herself, is facilitated by three things: the audible word, the presence of the object and our looking at the object.

This very same procedure is used in our instruction of the deaf and dumb, whose minds are well suited to the accurate identification of each letter as it reaches them, not through the portal of the ear, but rather through the eye, the window for visible images.

Then, when the deaf-mutes are shown the alphabet, they learn the various positions of the fingers which constitute the manual alphabet called dactylology by Péreire and arranged so that each letter is unique and easily distinguishable from the others.

That which Latin scholars call *littaras appelare*, the French call *épeler* and the Germans call *buchstabieren* [spelling] is done, not with the voice, but with the positioning of the fingers app-ropriate to each letter, an aptitude attained in one hour by diligent students and in two by the less diligent. To quote Horace, "That which reaches it through the ear makes a weaker impression on the heart than that which appears to that proven witness the eye, and the words of the observer himself" [Ars Poetica].

Allow me to exemplify. I write the word "window" on the board and point it out to a deaf-mute who uses the position of the fingers for each of the six letters three, four, or at most five times to memorize them while still looking at the word. He can then reproduce the written word without having to look at it.

He has committed the word to memory by paying close attention to the letters of it and their correct order. He will not forget it, because this word will occur in conversations conducted in systematized signs as well as in the classroom.

Let me mention in passing that the above described process takes no longer than two minutes, even for the beginner, under the guidance of a teacher.

Once the deaf-mutes have mastered the dactylology of the twenty-five letters of the French alphabet, we proceed to another vital task.

At first, the pupil's aptitude is of little importance. When he learns to write, we guide his hand for the first few days and let his own eyes be his teacher. The teacher is little concerned with faults in penmanship as long as the letters are readily distinguishable from one another, for the conjugation of verbs, the declination of nouns does not require pretty penmanship as long as the endings are clearly discernible. The students apply their efforts fully to this task by the second day at the latest.

Each day the students practice two or three temporal forms of a given verb using a grammar table. They then write the correct forms on the blackboard without consulting the table and after approximately seven days they have committed to memory all forms of the verb *porter.* Having mastered the pattern not only by seeing it, but also by imprinting it on their minds, they are now able to use the proper temporal and modal forms of all verbs of the same conjugation, both in writing and in systematized sign language.

The enthusiasm with which the children embark upon this assignment is unimaginable, unless they are still at an age were play is their only source of pleasure and have not yet come to appreciate the gratification of being able to gradually emerge from the abyss of darkness and engage in lively social intercourse with their fellows.

Further we teach them the basic principles of religion through brief series of questions, the systematically signed answers to which the students memorize and write on the board the next day. They are moved to tears of joy by this and we, too, sometimes lose our composure.

Directly following the first months of individual exercises, the students are admitted to the public classes held twice a week. Here they receive valuable practice in systematized signing, for the teacher dictates relevant material in the form of questions and answers and presented with the aid of systematized signs. In all, some four hundred words are chalked in boldface on a five-foot slate, which is then stood in front of the fifty students while the words are explained.

After we have said a prayer in systematized signs, we proceed to the explanation of each of the words in the questions. They are repeated perhaps ten times, either by the teacher or one of the more proficient students to the rest of the class. Having watched, the younger and less proficient pupils take turns at producing the signs. These signs not only describe the meaning of every single word, but also its exact grammatical form: its tense, mode, its gender and case. The proper signs for adverbs, conjunctions and prepositions are not neglected.

(The newcomer to these lessons is only required to remember

the signs for commonly used nouns.)

Thus, in the course of one month, three thousand words or more are reviewed and repeated in the demonstration classes. Most of these words are indelibly imprinted on the minds of the students. In that the students´ command of these words is reinforced through daily use, they will never forget them.

Far be it from us, learned Sir, to torment souls created in the image of God and capable of all higher knowledge by subjecting them to twelve or even fifteen months of mere speech training, as though the charges entrusted to our care were not human beings but insensible beasts.

How could we leave them in pitious ignorance of the revelations of the existence of God, the fundamental mysteries of religion and the Holy Sacrament? If not fulfill the Sacrament we must at least teach them enough so that, when they one day depart from this earthly life, they can enter the hereafter cleansed and quickened by the grace given to us by our Lord Jesus Christ!

Whatever objections Péreire may have to it, a teaching method which more quickly utilizes and develops the inborn strength of the soul is superior to one which does not dispell the darkness concealing the spirit until a year or more has past.

If, indeed, this process were free and easy, I do not deny that its length would be excusable. The student, however, is led onto a long, rough path of boredom and tedium, starting with tasks quite strenuous to the beginner. This could be more bearable if only it were interspersed with other exercises, more nourishing to the mind and progressing toward enlightenment. But oh! Agony! The hours are devoted solely to speech. There is as yet no time for thinking. While the tongue is freed, the mind is held prisoner in darkness.

What can the the best of teachers do in this situation but the job of the simple school master, a thing anyone could do if we were not so interested in impressing the inexperienced public? This aspect of instruction requires no great intellectual gifts; our dormitory matrons do a decent job of it on the young girls with whom they share quarters when we alot a few days to this mechanical task. What is needed here is patience; not an inquisitive mind.

If teachers and students devote more than two hours a day, one in the morning and another in the afternoon, to this ungratifying work, which Péreire thinks takes twelve or fifteen months to complete successfully, they are both exhausted and realize how tedious this method is. How should a student whose mind is put to so little use spend the rest of his day? He will be unbearably bored, he will yawn and find the days drag along very slowly unless he plays tricks and joins in frivolous games, because, without the guidance of a teacher, he is incapable of accomplishing anything worthwhile.

As I have already said, we nourish the pupil´s mind from the start and continue to do so throughout his education.

Péreire, unchallenged, never founded his method on any solid ground and for twenty-four years went on undisturbed as the sole proprietor of his invention. Indeed, when I challenged him in my *Instruction of the Mute* published in 1775, he declared his willingness to meet my criticism as soon as he had time. He never did. What a triumph it would have been to him, had he been able to foresee that you would become a champion of the same cause!

Before I continue to discuss this matter, erudite Sir, I beg to assure you that it is not my intention to confuse your method of teaching speech with that of Péreire, for with neither am I thoroughly familiar .

Your views do, however, coincide with his in the contention

that deaf-mutes should learn to speak before learning anything else. I have already attempted to explain my opposition to this view and shall now continue to answer your reproaches.

You say, "words, be they printed or hand written, look like a cluster of fly´s or spider´s legs and have no definite configuration to guide our imagination in the recollection of them when we no longer see them. One can hardly conjure a mental image of a single letter, much less a whole word."

Your example to prove this is the image of the word, "Paris", which you claim leaves no clear impression, remaining as legible as if written on a map or slate, once the eyes are closed. You are willing to stake a thousand to one on the mind´s inability to "paint" a picture of this word in its entirety.

You, then, set so little store by that wonderful and almost divine invention, the alphabet, celebrated by the most renowned of authors, that you do not hesitate to liken its letters to clusters of fly´s and spider´s legs.

It would not have surprised me, had Péreire dreamed up such an unheard of motivation for his method. It would have suited it well to have been founded on such a fallacy.

You, though, hold all previous methods in contempt as not only useless, but also extremely detrimental to the deaf-mute´s development. You announce a new method, taking for yourself all credit for its invention and expecting all teachers of the deaf-and-dumb to abandon their own methods in favor of yours. What road to wisdom do you open to us that we should trust you to lead the way? I would not have guessed, had not your baffling comparison divulged the secret of your invention.

You call your method new, but neither Péreire, nor his seniors, Amman and Bonet, would have agreed with you.

One day, when our debate is publicized, it is I who bet you a thousand to one that all men of learning and reason will oppose you.

You take for granted, erudite Sir, however you offer no proof, that the form of each written letter is not such that one of them cannot be confused with the other. The deaf-mutes themselves are my witnesses to the contrary. On the very first day of school, the majority of them form such a clear mental image of the form of each letter that when the chart from which they have learned the letters is removed from view, every one of the students can distinguish between them using the hand alphabet. [...] What more can you ask? As soon as they have been shown your word "Paris" and it has been erased, they will write it as soon as they come across a piece of chalk and slate or, if no writing material is at hand, express the word with the finger positions unique to each letter in the right order.

Regard, if you will, learned Sir, the large letters engraved above the portals of churches or public buildings. I find it hard to see there any likeness to a cluster of fly´s or spider´s legs. The characters leave such a viable impression on the mind that the natural imagination of any human being can easily reproduce them. For this reason, we, too, use large letters to begin with and then diminish them gradually. The mental images of the letters remain with the students whether we use large or small ones. Thus far, we have had no call to teach the small letters separately once the forms of the letters have been memorized.

You are willing to stake a thousand to one that the whole word "Paris" cannot be committed to memory. The truth of the matter is, however, if you will permit me to say so, you are laboring under a misconception. Removing the letters from their context, you conclude that they cannot be captured by the imagination, which you think capable of grasping only that which is physically present itself or shown in a picture.

Letters, however, be they printed or written, do not in fact appear separately and detached, but in the words of which they are components, each contributing with its unique characteristics to the whole. It is in this state that they constantly affect the imagination, whether we have seen them written in black or white. Thus they are clear and concise and as legible to the mind as when we see them on a map or in a book.

To better understand this, one must take into consideration the fact that our imagination is capable of creating images similar to those we have actually seen: images equally distinct as the actual object they depict. Our minds have eyes as sharp as those of our bodies.

Just as our eyes do not scramble the five letters of your example, our mind does not confuse one letter of a given word with another. We can create in our mind an image of that set of letters, be they made of gold, silver, iron, stone or wood, painted white or black, red or green, be the letters large or small. This natural capacity can be applied, not only to short words, but also longer ones, provided we have studied the words attentively and not just skimmed over them.

He who does not acknowledge this power has never put his imagination to use or tried its powers.

Just as our eyes can perceive an entire sentence more quickly than we can pronounce it, the words "Pavete Ad Sancturarium Meum: Ego Dominus" [Tremble Before My Sanctuary: I am the Lord] chiseled a half-foot high in stone above the portals of houses of God, are grasped by the mind faster than we are able to pronounce them.

Now we would like to see what you have to suggest in place of this easily comprehensible method. Allow me to quote from your letter in the Latin translation: "My pupils learn", you say, "the art of reading and repeating the sounds of the words in a loud voice, distinctly and with understanding. In their waking hours and in their dreams they think in their articulated language. Whoever so wishes can speak to them, provided he pronounces his words slowly. To their minds the written language is based on the sounds of the language, which, it is true, they do not hear, but perceive with another sense: a difference of no inherent importance. At first they harp a sorrowful one-note melody, but after two or three years they speak clearly and distinctly and finally they even learn the art of declamation."

I claim then, returning once more to your example, that my deaf-mutes perceive the word "Paris" in a single moment, so that, once it is erased, they can reproduce it even more promptly; while your pupils cannot retain the word in their memory until you have instructed them as to which position the throat, the tongue, the teeth, the lips and the cheeks should assume in order to pronounce each of the letters of the word. Having pronounced the word, however, they cannot themselves determine whether their pronunciation is correct, for they cannot hear the sounds you utter.

Assuming — I assume, not concede — that your students have achieved considerable success in articulation, they will not be able to recall a given word later without going through the motions of articulating the individual sounds of each of its letters in the way described above and in the order in which they occur in the word, and will only be able to assure themselves that they are pronouncing the word correctly by feeling the touch of their tongue on other parts of the mouth. This is obviously a long and tedious process.

You claim your students, whether awake or dreaming, think in their articulated language. I frankly confess that I have no clue as to what is meant by "thinking in one's articulated language". A Frenchman, you mean, dreams in French, a speaker of Latin in Latin, a German in German; but more often than not, I dream in no language at all, for very frequently the things that appear to me in dreams, being figments of the imagination, have no names in the languages I know. It also happens at times that I dream of things the correct names for which I do not know, like the myriad of craftsmen's tools: gadgets I have no doubt seen, but never heard named. As regards other objects whose names I certainly know, it happens quite often that they occupy my mind in dreams without my being able to recall their names in any language known to me. Nor is it any wonder that, even when I am awake, I often think with rapt attention and great fondness of things or people whose names, try as I might, I simply cannot bring to mind.

I find it reassuring, learned Sir, though not in the least surprising, to hear that your pupils learn to speak clearly and finally to declaim in two or three years. At the end of my *Instruction* you will indeed find a five page speech in Latin which was presented in his own mode of oration by one of our deaf-and-dumb-born students before a large, specially invited audience.

Now to the third point of contention between us. You believe it is impossible for the deaf-and-dumb to recall and write down all the words expressing our thoughts as soon as they see them presented in systematized sign, either by the teacher, a classmate or someone else.

You must keep in mind that we do not deal with all the words of the language but only with those commonly used, be it in the circle of the family, in our private or public religion classes, or indeed in some randomly chosen book of edifying content. All the terms of the advanced sciences, of arts and crafts are not learned by the deaf-mute at all or are only encountered by coincidence when they are used by his teacher. It is, then, no wonder if he soon forgets them again. It is enough for him to commit to memory the words most men find sufficient for a righteous life.

Visitors from all over the world, whom I could not fool even if I wanted to, can confirm that I dictate all of these essential words to the deaf-mutes in systematized signs, from an open book or a newly opened letter. Every day, sceptics come to our school, incredulous of our reputation; when they leave us, they are sceptics no longer. I have indeed encountered no one in all these years whose doubts have been confirmed by a visit to our school.

Allow me to cite one of these thousands of witnesses, that is Péreire himself, who, after seeing me dictate a letter he had given me to a deaf-mute in systematized signs, exclaimed in astonishment, "Had I not seen it with my own eyes, I would never have believed it!"

Please consider that Péreire could also have dictated this letter to his pupils, the difference between his approach and mine being that he would have spelled each word to them dactylologically. His students would be able to reproduce the words correctly on paper, but would not comprehend the meaning inherent in those lines of characters.

Systematized signs, however, do not belong to any one language and denote neither word nor letter; but rather express concepts. Once the student has grasped these concepts he can express them in whatever his own language may be and with all types of words. There is no danger whatsoever of his not understanding his own words.

His Imperial Majesty understood the difference between these two methods of dictation when I dictated these German words to one of my female students in dactylology: *"Es sei ferne von mir, dass ich mich rühme, denn allein in dem Kreuz..."* [Gal. 6:14:

"But far be it from me to glory except in the cross..."] When I asked the girl to explain in systematized signs the meaning of the words, she replied that she had not understood them. The Kaiser then realized how mechanical this method is and that the same reply can be expected in whichever language the words are dictated dactylologically to the deaf-mutes.

Do not let this lead you to conclude, however, that we discard dactylology completely. We use it where it is necessary, that is, to indicate the names of persons, countries, cities. These arbitrary labels cannot be expressed in systematized signs.

Still another sample of our art was demonstrated to his Imperial Majesty: placing five deaf-mutes so that none could see what the others were writing, I dictated to them an excerpt from one of our previous exercises, a sentence approximately ten words long, in systematized signs. One of the pupils reproduced the sentence in French, a second in Latin, a third in Italian, a fourth in Spanish, and the fifth in English. This did not surprise the kaiser either, but demonstrated to him that my signs depict neither letters nor words; only concepts, a thing common to all countries and languages and, once understood, easily expressed in the respective mother tongues.

You may conclude from this description, learned Sir (please forgive my digressing somewhat from the issues under debate), that I rightly claim that systematized signs could provide the universal language long sought after by the learned: a system by which people of different nationalities could meet and make themselves understood to one another, and could record lectures in the words of their respective languages. This could be achieved if in all schools, on order of the nations´ leaders — Abbé de Condillac expressed this wish in his time — no teacher or professor ever used a word for which he had not taught the students the systematized sign.

I will however not deny the complication pointed out to me by many learned men: the fact that it would not be feasible to accomodate for the word order of every idiom while presenting a sentence in systematized signs. Furthermore, the structures of various languages are said to vary so greatly that a person applying the word order of the French language to an utterance in systematized signs could hardly expect an Italian, let alone a German, to understand its sense.

Quite on the contrary, the viewers here can reasonably be assumed to have been schooled from an early age and to be as thoroughly familiar with systematized signs as the Frenchman is with his French or the German with his German. In such a case one could observe a phenomenon similar to what would happen if one were to dictate a sentence in French to a group of twelve Frenchmen well versed in Latin and request that they translate it into Latin. None of these twelve would dream of retaining the word order of spoken French in his Latin version and one can be equally sure that no two of the twelve translations would be identical in word order or phrasing. No educated translator would strive to preserve the word order of the French; instead, his ambition would be to duplicate the meaning of the entire sentence as closely as possible.

This would also be the case when translating from systematized signs into any language. The order in which the gestures are presented is of little interest. Much more important to any conscientious translator is arranging the concepts thus presented in a way permitted by the conventions of his own spoken or written language.

At the end of your letter, erudite Sir, you mention having taught two hundred deaf-mutes to speak and that these have become, not only worthy members of human society but also highly skilled artists and craftsmen. But what thanks is this proficiency to us? Through apprenticeship, our deaf-mutes can learn virtually any craft from skilled masters without our intervention. Indeed it sometimes happens that some inborn talent takes the place of a teacher and such gifted people excel far beyond those who have completed apprenticeships.

You are fortunate to be the subject of a ruler who shows such benevolence toward your institution, one who not only grants you an annuary of four hundred *Thaler*, but who also provides you with living quarters and what firewood you need as a suplement to your daily income from the practice of your art.

As for me, I have, since birth been showered with such gifts by Providence, that even those most charitably and philan-thropically inclined toward me would scold me were I not to give to others that which I too have received as a gift.

I could, then, never advise the teacher of the deaf and dumb in Vienna to devote his own energy to teaching speech, but rather that he train teachers for this mechanical task under his guidance and that he in the meantime devote his efforts to more useful and important subjects.

In conclusion, learned Sir, however large the gulf between our opinions, it cannot diminish the esteem I forever harbor for you.

Your obedient servant,

The teacher of the deaf and dumb in Paris

Samuel Heinicke´s Reply to Abbé de l'Épée´s Second Letter

Reverend and Highly Esteemed Sir,

Although it was a great honor and pleasure for me to receive your letter of recently, I must frankly confess that our views on the best approach to the instruction of the deaf and dumb differ vastly and I doubt very much that you and I will ever reach a common goal.

If my memory serves me correctly, I have told you earlier that I know well, not only your method, but that of everyone else who has made a contribution to the area of educating the deaf and dumb. I have also already mentioned that I used the finger alphabet in my own teaching twenty years ago, but noticed at once that, with regard to intelligibility as well as the ability of the students to recall what they have learned through it, it does not compare with the method I have devised and practice. My method is based on articulated and vocalized language and the sense of taste which replaces the absent sense of hearing.

If I am to discuss my teaching method with you, you must have experienced it first hand and learned it directly from me. To this end, you must come to my city and spend at least six months here.

In no way is my method congruent with that used by Péreire, Deschamps and other certainly significant scholars, except perhaps in the area of written language and then only insofar as a text is regarded as a copy or imitation of articulated, vocalized language.

Articulated language is the essence of my method of

educating the deaf-and-dumb. It is through articulated language, and the ideas associated with it, that the students acquire a larger store of concepts and experience, enabling them to cross from the realm of the empirical into the realm of the intellectual. Through experiences afforded them by art [the conditioned association of taste sensations with sounds of the language] they acquire the associative ability which constitutes the main-spring affected by affinities and aversions and combining to create the capacity for independent thought and action in the deaf-mutes themselves. I have discussed this subject in much greater depth in my *Beobachten über Stumme* [Reflections on Muteness] written in German and published in Hamburg in the year 1778 by the bookdealer Herold.

Step by step, my dumb pupils learn, without great difficulty, to speak their native language and also foreign languages loudly and clearly, with the comprehension and deportment of those blessed with hearing. Moreover they are suited to a variety of skills and to the understanding of all fields of sci-ence, with the single exception of an animate and genuine grasp of sounds, of which they can only obtain a partial and shadowy understanding for example by likening them to the ripples on water.

Not only do my pupils ponder the arts and sciences, but you will also find it possible to discuss such subjects with them in a living language and you can dictate what you will for them to write. These facts are known, not only here, but everywhere and have been verified by many dignitaries and learned men.

Were you to believe I do not at all utilize finger-language in my instruction you would be fundamentally mistaken. However, I use it only to form concepts; the signs used by my students to communicate ideas are sounds and written letters.

At present only I and my sons know this method devised by

me for the instruction of the deaf-and-dumb. It has cost me much sweat; unbelievable exertion has gone into its creation and perfection. For this reason I have no intention of teaching it to others at some ridiculously low price.

I would only sell it to some royal house for a princely fortune and I challenge any pedant to try to wrench it from me by disputation. Poor deaf-mutes are instructed by me free of charge and rich ones are charged according to the size of their fortune. I often receive more than I have demanded.

I wish you well, esteemed Sir, and may you remain in good health.

Leipzig, With the highest regards on July 12, 1782.

S. Heinicke

Abbé de l'Épée´s Third and Last letter to Samuel Heinicke

Dear Learned and Esteemed Sir,

Had you not opposed my method, which has also been adopted by the Viennese teacher of the the deaf and dumb, calling it useless and detrimental to the progress of the pupils, I should never have thought of comparing my method with yours. My role in our dispute has been a defensive one, rather than that of the aggressor.

I do not, however, cease to wonder at your unsolicited offer, expressed by you in the following words: "If I am to discuss my teaching method with you, you must have experienced it first hand and learned it directly from me. To this end, you must come to my city and spend at least six months here."

Do not be angry with me, esteemed Sir, for refusing your voluntary offer.

I am not in need of six months of instruction in a skill it would take me at most a fortnight to teach the simplest of our governesses for the deaf and dumb.

Let this much be said of your exclusive method, learned Sir, supposedly known only to you and your very dear sons: I will not learn it in your presence or that of your emissary; I will teach it to any sensible hearing man.

I have not ventured to comment on this topic in my previous letters, uncertain as to how you actually went about teaching speech. Now, however, you yourself have unveiled your secret by saying, "My method is based on articulated and vocalized language and the sense of taste which replaces the absent sense of hearing."

I too tread no other path, with the one exception that I do not refer to the inner contact of the various tools of speech as "taste"; nor would that label appeal to scientists, taste being one of the five senses, good only for distinguishing one flavor from another. It has not as yet been ascertained whether the sense of taste is located mainly in the tongue or in the palate. Most likely, it is, as we observe from daily experience, equally divided between both.

Further, all contact with the tools of speech does not give any sensation of taste, but merely a tactile stimulus not at all related to flavor.

It is then our duty to arouse the tactile sensations in the deaf-and-dumb, to draw their attention to them again and again, until they become so accustomed to inducing the same sensations themselves that they can do so without assistance.

To this end, we need neither a silver instrument nor one of gold. Let Péreire keep this useless gadget, the only purpose of which is to deceive the inexperienced. We attain the desired results with our hands and fingers, using them at the appropriate moments in the appropriate places. We do not do this behind closed doors as that gentleman did, but in front of as many witnesses as may happen to be present. While demonstrating our lessons, we give our observers instructions as to how they might apply what they learn here to the speech instruction of deaf and dumb pupils at home who are unable to attend our classes themselves.

From this you can conclude, erudite Sir, how little I would benefit from a visit to you in Leipzig.

One more thing does frankly astonish me. That is that you admit in the letter I recently received from you that you do use finger-language to combine concepts. The word is your own.

To any man of reason, this simple confession is proof enough of the fact that your exercises are nothing but purely mechanical ones: that you do not compare ideas to one another, but words to words and letters to letters, for dactylology is nothing but the presentation of letters with varying positions of the fingers, with which the words of any language can be spelled without in any way divulging their meaning.

It follows that, when a teacher dictates to them using dactylology, the pupils will faithfully reproduce on paper the letters represented by the positions of the fingers, working as speedily as the organist upon the keys of his instrument. They will, however, remain in the dark as to the sense of what they are writing. Similarly, they can learn to produce appropriate answers to the questions put to them without at all grasping their answers. Although they will seem well educated, in reality they will be nothing but faithful scribes.

I wish you well-being, learned Sir, with all my heart. If the distance between us were only a few miles, I should be more than happy to pay you a visit.

Your most humble and obedient servant,

The Teacher of the Deaf and Dumb in Paris

List of Literature

Amman, J.C. (1694).
The Talking Deaf Man. London. Kungliga biblioteket, Stockholm.

Andersson, B.. (1987).
Myter i dagsljus. Förnuft och oförnuft i handikapphistorien. Bokförlaget Inferi, Bollnäs.

Andersson, E. & Ekholm, C. (1988).
Teckenspråksundervisning i Sverige och övriga Norden. Publikationer från institutionene för pedagogik, 1988:21. FUVUX-projektet. Institutionen för pedagogik, Göteborgs universitet.

Andersson, L. (1990).
Dövutbildning i Frankrike före Milanokongressen - en kortfattad redogörelse för dövutbildningens framväxt i Frankrike före 1900. Institutionen f. lingvistik, Göteborgs universitet.

Bergman, B. (1977).
Tecknad svenska. Utbildningsforskning. SÖ rapport 28. Skolöverstyrelsen.

Blomkvist, J. (1875).
Om döfstum-bildningen i Sverige af Jehubba P. Blomkvist, lärare vid allmänna institutet för döfstumma och blinda. Stockholm.

Blomkvist, J. (1875).
Om läroanstalter för döfstumma med särskilt hänseende till tal- och språkundervisningen af Jehubba Blomkvist, föreståndare för Örebro läns döfstumskola. Stockholm.

Blomkvist, J. (1899).
Om döfstumbildningen i Sverige. Handskrivet koncept, Birgittaskolans arkiv, Örebro.

Campbell, D. (1732).
Secret Memoirs of the Late Duncan Campbell etx, Deaf and Dumb Gentleman etc, London. Kungliga biblioteket, Stockholm.

Ciba-Journalen. (1948).
Dövstumheten. Nummer 18. Band 2. Basel, september 1948.

Czech, F.H. (1948).
Versinnlichte Denk- und Spracklehre, mit Anwendung auf die Religions- und Settenlehre und auf das Leben. Wien.

Dalsjö, M. (1906).
Valda skrifter av Platon i svensk översättning av Magnus Dalsjö. Sjunde delen Kratylos. Stockholm.

Degsell, C. (1981).
Vad sa kyrkofadern Augustinus egentligen? Dövas kyrkoblad 1981, nr 2.

DeLand, F. (1931).
The Story of Lip-Reading, its Genesis and Development by Fred DeLand, Superintendent of the Volta Bureau 1914 - 1922.

Deschamps, C. F. (1779)
Cours Élémentaire d´Education des Sourds et Muets. Manillaskolan, Stockholm.

Dialekt- och Ortnamnsarkivet i Lund. (1990).
Brev.

Døv Informasjon. (1990).
Døves Forlag A.S., Bergen, Norge.

Emmerig, E. (1927).
Bilderatlas zur Geschichte der Taubstummenbildung. Manillaskolan, Stockholm.

Farrar, A. (1923).
Arnold on the Education of the Deaf. London.

Fay, E.A. (1893).
Histories of American Schools for the Deaf, 1817 - 1893. Volume I. The Volta Bureau, Washington D.C.

Grimberg, C. (1927)
Världshistoria. Folkens liv och kultur. Fortiden II. P.A. Norstedt & Söners Förlag, Stockholm.

Guyot, R.T. (1824).
Dissertatio Juridica Inauguralis De Iure Surdo-Mutorum. Auctorer Rembto, Tobia Guyot, Groningen, Holland.

Holder, W. (1669).
Elements of Speech: Deaf & Dumb. London. Kungliga biblioteket, Stockholm.

The Holy Bible
Revised Standard Version 1946 and 1953, Collins Press, New York, USA.

The Holy Qur´an. (1988.)
English translation by S. V. Mir Ahmed Als. Tahrike Tarsile Quran, Elmhurst, N.Y. USA.

Keller, J. (1867).
Nordisk tidskrift for blinde-, døvstumme- och idiotskolen. Kjøbenhavn.

Kierkegaard-Ekbohrn, C. (1881).
Kongressen af Döf-stumlärare i Milano. Tidskrift för döfstumskolan. N:o 1. Andra årgången.

Kruth, L. (1972).
Sveriges Dövas Riksförbunds jubileumshäfte 50 år.

Kungliga biblioteket.
Uppsatser om de l´Épées liv. Handskriftssektionen. Pär Aron Borgs arkiv.

La Rochelle, E. (1882).
Jacob Rodrigues Péreire. Premier instituteur des sourds-muets en France. Sa vie et ses travaux. Par Ernest La Rochelle. De la biblioteque nationale, Paris. Société d´imprimerie Paul Dupont, 41, Rue Jean-Jaques-Rousseau. 1882.

Lindfors, O.A. (1830).
Handbok i romerska antiqviteterna. N.M. Linch förlag, Örebro.

Moser, H.M. (1958).
Handsignals: Finger-Spelling. Technical Note No. 49. Contract No. AF 19 (604) - 1577. The Ohio State University Research Foundation, Columbus 8, Ohio, USA.

Nyström, A.F. (1900).
Grunddragen af Döfstumundervisningens utveckling i Sverige. Örebro.

Nyström, A.F. (1906).
Den cerebro-induktiva läsemetoden eller ordmetoden jämte fragment ur bokstafveringsmetodens och ljudmetodens historia av A.F. Nyström, lärare vid dövstumlärareseminariet Manilla, Stockholm.

Nyström, A.F. (1907).
Handbok i dövstumundervisningens allmänna historia.

Nyström, A.F. (1919).
Olika folk och deras ställning under olika tider. P. Alfr. Persons Förlag, Uppsala.

Peringskiöld, J. (1697).
Emund Lagmans i Sveriges Historia. Heimskringla eller Snorre Sturlasons Nordländska Konungasagor...edit...I-II. Stockholm. Lunds universitet.

Richardin. (1834).
Réflexions et citations sur l´état moral des sourds-muets sans instruction sur celui des sourds-muets qu´on instruit.

Reuschert, W. (1881).
Heilpädagogische Karte. Entworfen und gezeichnet von W. Reuschert, ordentl. Lehrer an der Kaiserl. Taubstummen-Anstalt zu Metz. Metz 1881. Planscher.

Schumann, G. & Schumann, P. (1912).
Samuel Heinickes gesammelte Schriften. Herausgeben von Georg und Paul Schumann. Ernst Wiebandt, Verlagsbuchhandlung, Leipzig.

Schyberg, S. (1975).
Birgittaskolan 100 år, 1875-1975. Kort historik. Örebro.

Sourd et al. (1990).
Le Pouvoir des Signes. Institut National de Jeunes Sourds de Paris.

SDR-Kontakt. (1990).
Nr 7. Världens första professur i teckenspråk inrättas 1 juli.

SDR-Kontakt. (1991).
Nr 8. Tema EG.

SOU. (1947:64).
Betänkande och förslag rörande dövstummundervisningen avgivet av 1945 års dövstumutredning. Ecklesiastikdepartementet.

SOU. (1955:20).
Det döva barnets språk- och talutveckling. Betänkande avgivet av utredningen rörande de nya vetenskapliga rönen på audiologiens och audiometriens område i vården av döva barn. Stockholm.

Svenska akademiens ordbok. (1923).

Sveriges Dövas Riksförbund. (1990).
Förbundsnytt, sommaren 1990.

Tidskrift för döfstumskolan. (1880).
Inbjudning till 1880 års internationella kongress för förbättrande af de döfstummas ställning. N:o 3. Första årgången.

Valade-Gabel, J.J. (1863).
Le mot et l'image. Premier livre des sourds-muets. Paris.

Wallisii, I (1765).
Grammatica linguae Anglicanae, cui praefigitur de loquela sive de sonorum amnium loquelarium formatione etc. Kungliga biblioteket, Stockholm.

Widell, J. (1988).
Den danske døvekultur. Bind II. Danske Døves Landsforbund, København.

Wilén, J.A. (1886).
Upplysningar och råd. Informationsskrift. J.A. Wilén, föreståndare för döfstumskolan i Uppsala. Landsarkivet i Göteborg; Vänerskolans handlingar.

von der Lieth, L. (1967).
Dansk døve-tegnsprog. I kommision hos akademisk forlag, København 1967.

Wright, D. (1969).
Deafness, a Personal Account. Allentane the Penguin Press, London.

Wågström-Lundquist, G. (1990).
TV-programmet "Under samma himmel". Utbildningsradion.

Zommarin, H.
Anteckningar av Hilding Zommarin, rektor vid dövskolan i Örebro 1934 - 1965.

Åberg, A. (1967).
Tid och rum, världshistorisk atlas. Generalstabens Litografiska Anstalts Förlag, Stockholm.

Åberg, K. (1982).
Bibelkonkordans till Nya testamentet 1981. SkeabVerbum.

Österberg, O. (1925).
Tystnadens folk. P Alfr. Persons Förlag, Uppsala.

Index of Names

Index of Illustrations

Information: Bilderatlas = Bilderatlas zur Geschichte der Taubstummenbildung.
E. Emmerig, 1927. Manilla School for the Deaf in
Stockholm, Sweden
Ciba = Dövstumheten. Ciba-Journalen, no 18, Basel, september 1948.
Novaritis Läkemedel, Sverige AB, Box 115, SE-183 11 Täby, Sweden.

The cover shows the oldest known color wall chart of the finger-spelling alphabet,
Vadstena School for Older Deaf Students 1878 to 1902. National Archives, Vadstena,
Sweden.